I0439719

Informing the legislative debate since 1914 _____

Export-Import Bank: Overview and Reauthorization Issues

Shayerah Ilias Akhtar

Specialist in International Trade and Finance

June 30, 2014

Congressional Research Service

7-5700

www.crs.gov

R43581

Summary

The Export-Import Bank of the United States (Ex-Im Bank or the Bank), an independent federal government agency, is the official export credit agency (ECA) of the United States. It operates under a renewable charter, the Export-Import Bank Act of 1945 (P.L. 79-173), as amended. Ex-Im Bank helps finance U.S. exports of manufactured goods and services, with the objective of contributing to U.S. employment, in circumstances when alternative financing is not available or to assist U.S. exporters to meet foreign, government-backed sponsored, export credit competition. Its main programs are direct loans, loan guarantees, working capital finance, and export credit insurance. Its transactions are backed by the full faith and credit of the U.S. government.

Legislation was enacted in the 112th Congress to extend Ex-Im Bank's authority through the close of business on September 30, 2014 (P.L. 112-122) and to raise its exposure cap (total amount of outstanding credit and insurance authority) to $140 billion by FY2014. Currently, Congress is debating whether to renew Ex-Im Bank's authority and, if so, for how long and under what terms.

Background

Congress sets statutory requirements for Ex-Im Bank's support in its charter, under which the Bank's financing must have a reasonable assurance of repayment and must supplement, and not compete with, private capital. Ex-Im Bank also abides by international rules for government-backed export credit activity as a participant to the Organization for Economic Co-operation and Development (OECD) Arrangement on Officially Supported Export Credits.

In FY2013, Ex-Im Bank approved 3,842 transactions of finance and insurance support, which amounted to $27.3 billion in approved commitments, estimated by Ex-Im Bank to support $37.4 billion in U.S. exports of goods and services. Its overall portfolio exposure level in FY2013 was $113.8 billion—below the $130 billion statutory cap for that year. Following the 2008-2009 financial crisis, the Bank's exposure level has increased.

Ex-Im Bank uses offsetting collections to cover costs of its operations. As part of the annual appropriations process, Congress sets an upper limit on the level available to the Bank for operations and provides a direct appropriation for its Office of Inspector General (OIG). In terms of operating expenses, Ex-Im Bank has been "self-sustaining" for appropriations purposes since FY2008. For FY2014, Congress set an upper limit of $115.5 million for the Bank's administrative expenses, provided $5.1 million for its OIG, and allowed carryover funds of up to $10 million to remain available through FY2016. Ex-Im Bank provided $1.1 billion to the U.S. Treasury in FY2013 after covering operating expenses and loan loss reserves. Ex-Im Bank assesses credit and other risks of proposed transactions, monitors current commitments for risks, and maintains reserves against potential losses. Ex-Im Bank reports that its overall default rate as of March 31, 2014, was 0.211% and that, since 1992, its recovery rate has been 50 cents on the dollar on average for transactions in default.

Issues for Congress

Members of Congress hold a range of views on Ex-Im Bank. Proponents assert that the Bank supports U.S. exports by addressing market failures that dampen export levels and helps U.S. exporters compete against foreign companies backed by their governments' ECAs. Critics oppose the use of taxpayer funds for private benefit, whether for large or small businesses, and contend that the private sector is more efficient in financing exports. The Ex-Im Bank reauthorization issues facing Congress are two-fold. The first issue is whether to renew the Bank in its current form, or pursue alternatives, such as allowing its authority to expire or reorganizing its functions. In April 2014, the Obama Administration submitted a legislative proposal to Congress requesting a reauthorization of Ex-Im Bank. Second, should Congress choose to renew Ex-Im Bank's authority, specific reauthorization issues could include the following:

- *For how long should Ex-Im Bank be reauthorized?* A shorter renewal period, as provided in 2012, could allow for more active congressional oversight of Ex-Im Bank. A longer renewal, such as four to five years, typical of past reauthorizations, could enhance Ex-Im Bank's long-term planning and provide more assurance to those involved in Ex-Im Bank-supported transactions. The Administration's legislative proposal calls for a five-year renewal of the Bank's authority.

- *Should Ex-Im Bank's exposure cap be adjusted and if so, by what amount?* Congress has periodically raised the Bank's exposure cap. Given growing demand for Ex-Im Bank's services, some call for an increase in the Bank's exposure limit. Critics have, in part, opposed raising the cap based on concerns about Ex-Im Bank's risk management practices, and may favor maintaining or lowering the cap. The Administration's legislative proposal asks for the cap to be raised incrementally to $160 billion by FY2018.

- *What revisions should be made to Ex-Im Bank's policies, if any?* Debate could center on the Bank's effectiveness and efficiency in meeting its core export and jobs mission and other statutory requirements, as well as international concerns, including the policies of foreign ECAs. Concerns about the competitiveness of the Bank's policies relative to foreign ECAs may be weighed against the Bank's efforts to balance a range of stakeholder interests, including those representing business, labor, and environmental concerns.

- *How well does the Bank manage the risks associated with its portfolio?* Focus on the Bank's risk management practice has grown since the financial crisis, as its exposure level has increased. Key areas of focus include the Bank's analytic tools for risk management, as well as its operational capacity to manage its growing portfolio prudentially. Questions also may be raised about whether the cost of federal credit is priced appropriately.

- *How should the United States approach international disciplines to guide government-backed export credit activity?* For some stakeholders, the growth in unregulated financing by U.S. trading partners has raised questions about the effectiveness of the OECD Arrangement and what role the World Trade Organization may play in establishing export credit disciplines. It also has prompted consideration of efforts to bring China and other non-OECD countries into the Arrangement, as well as U.S. efforts to negotiate separate export credit disciplines with China. Others call for enhanced U.S. efforts to eliminate all international government-backed export financing through negotiations in the OECD and other venues.

Contents

Figures

Tables

Appendixes

Contacts

The Export-Import Bank of the United States (Ex-Im Bank or the Bank) is an independent U.S. government executive agency and a wholly-owned U.S. government corporation.[1] It is the official export credit agency (ECA) of the United States, and is charged with financing and promoting exports of U.S. manufactured goods and services, with the objective of contributing to the employment of U.S. workers. Ex-Im Bank is among the federal government agencies involved in promoting U.S. exports of goods and services.[2]

The Bank operates under a renewable charter, the Export-Import Bank Act of 1945, as amended (P.L. 79-173; 12 U.S.C. §635 et seq.). In 2012, Congress debated and ultimately reauthorized Ex-Im Bank through the close of business on September 30, 2014 (P.L. 112-122). Currently, Congress is considering whether to renew Ex-Im Bank's authority and if so, for how long and under what terms.

This report provides (1) a general background of Ex-Im Bank; (2) a discussion of the international context of the Bank; (3) analysis of key issues that Congress may consider in a reauthorization debate; and (4) the congressional outlook on Ex-Im Bank.

Background

Ex-Im Bank seeks to (1) correct market failures by assuming the risks of financing exports that the private sector is unwilling, or unable, to undertake alone at competitive terms; and/or (2) meet foreign competition by countering government-backed financing offered by other countries to their companies.[3]

Overview of Ex-Im Bank Policies

Congress sets statutory requirements for Ex-Im Bank's activity in its charter (see **Table 1** for summary). Under the charter, Ex-Im Bank's financing must have a reasonable assurance of repayment and must supplement, not compete with, private sources of financing. The charter also includes other statutory requirements that serve as the basis for Ex-Im Bank's policies, for example, with respect to providing terms that are fully competitive with other ECAs, economic and environmental considerations, and focusing on supporting specific types of exports.

Ex-Im Bank also abides by the Organization for Economic Cooperation and Development (OECD) Arrangement on Officially Supported Export Credits (the "Arrangement"), which establishes terms and conditions for the export credit agencies of the United States and other participants (discussed later).

---

[1] A U.S. government corporation is a government agency established by Congress to provide market-oriented public services and to produce revenues that meet or approximate expenditures. See CRS Report RL30365, *Federal Government Corporations: An Overview*, by Kevin R. Kosar.

[2] For more information, see CRS Report R41495, *U.S. Government Agencies Involved in Export Promotion: Overview and Issues for Congress*, coordinated by Shayerah Ilias Akhtar.

[3] Ex-Im Bank, *Annual Report 2013 of the Export-Import Bank of the United States* (hereinafter Ex-Im Bank, *FY2013 Annual Report*), http://www.exim.gov/about/library/reports/annualreports/2013/.

Table 1. Overview of Major Statutory and Policy Requirements for Ex-Im Bank

Requirement	Description	Statutory Basis
OVERALL		
Mandate	Ex-Im Bank's mandate is to support financing and to facilitate U.S. exports of goods and services and, in doing so, contribute to the employment of U.S. workers.	12 U.S.C. 635(a)(1)
Private Capital	The Bank must supplement and encourage, and not compete with, private capital.	12 U.S.C. 635(b)(1)(B)
Reasonable Assurance of Repayment	All Ex-Im Bank transactions must have a reasonable assurance of repayment.	2 U.S.C. 635(b)(1)(B)
Rates, Terms, and Conditions	Ex-Im Bank loans must be at rates and on terms and conditions which are fully competitive with exports of other countries, and consistent with international agreements.	12 U.S.C 635(b)(1)(B)
Fees	The Bank is authorized to charge fees and premiums commensurate with the risks covered in connection with its contractual liability for its financing.	12 U.S.C. 635(c)(1)
Due Diligence	The Bank is required to set due diligence standards for its lender partners and participants.	12 U.S.C. 635(i)
Exposure Cap	Congress sets a limitation on the total amount of outstanding loans, guarantees, and insurance Ex-Im Bank can have any one time. For FY2014, the exposure cap is $140 billion.	12 U.S.C. 635e(F)(ii)
Default Rate	Ex-Im Bank must monitor its default rate; report quarterly to Congress on its default rate; and, if the default rate exceeds 2%, submit a report to Congress on a plan to reduce it to below 2%.	12 U.S.C. 635g(g)
TRANSACTION-SPECIFIC		
Content	Content is the amount of domestic and foreign costs from labor, materials, overhead, and other inputs associated with the production of an export. Based on its jobs mandate, the Bank finances the U.S. content of U.S. exports, which the agency considers to be a proxy for U.S. jobs. For medium- and long-term transactions, Ex-Im Bank limits its support to the lesser of: (1) 85% of the value of all goods and services contained within a U.S. supply contract or; (2) 100% of the U.S. content of an export contract. In effect, in order to receive full Ex-Im Bank financing for an export transaction, the minimum domestic content is 85% and the maximum foreign content allowance is 15%. If the foreign content exceeds 15%, then the Bank's support would be reduced proportionally. For short-term transactions, the minimum U.S. content required for full financing is generally 50%.	Ex-Im Bank policy
Local Cost	Local costs are the project-related costs for goods and services that are incurred in the buyer's country. When Ex-Im Bank provides medium- or long-term financing for U.S. exports for foreign projects, it may also provide local cost support. Specifically, the Bank can support up to 30% of the value of the U.S. exports for goods and services that are originated and/or manufactured in the buyer's country, subject to certain requirements.	Ex-Im Bank policy

Requirement	Description	Statutory Basis
Economic Impact	The Bank is required to have regulations and procedures to insure that full consideration is given to the extent that any loan or guarantee is likely to have an adverse effect on industries and employment in the United States. [12 U.S.C. 635a-2] These regulations and procedures are in support of the congressional policy that in authorizing any loan or guarantee the Board of Directors shall take into account any serious adverse effect of such loan or guarantee. [12 U.S.C. 635(b)(1)(B)] Furthermore, the Bank is prohibited from extending any loan or guarantee that would establish or expand the production of any commodity for export by any other country if the commodity is likely to be in surplus on world markets or the resulting production capacity will compete with U.S. production of a similar commodity and will cause "substantial injury" to U.S. producers of a similar commodity [12 U.S.C. 635(e)(1)]. The Bank defines risk of substantial injury as the extension of a loan or guarantee that will enable a foreign buyer to establish or expand foreign production by an amount that is equal to or greater than 1% of U.S. production. The same prohibition applies to loans or guarantees subject to U.S. trade measures, such as anti-dumping or countervailing duties. [12 U.S.C. 635(e)(2)] However, these prohibitions shall not apply if the Board of Directors determines that the proposed transaction's short- and long-term benefits to U.S. industry and U.S. employment are likely to outweigh the injury to U.S. producers and U.S. employment of similar commodities. [12 U.S.C. 635(e)(3)]	12 U.S.C. 635a-2; 12 U.S.C. 635(b)(1)(B); 12 U.S.C. 635(e)(1); 12 U.S.C. 635(e)(2); 12 U.S.C. 635(e)(3)
Environmental Impact	The Bank considers the potential beneficial or adverse environmental effects of proposed transactions. The Bank is authorized to grant or withhold financing support after taking into account the environmental impact of the proposed transaction.	12 U.S.C. 635i-5
U.S. Flag Shipping	Products supported by Ex-Im Bank exported via ships must be transported exclusively on U.S. flagged vessels. This requirement applies to any shipped exports receiving a direct loan from Ex-Im Bank, or any shipped export over $20 million that receives an Ex-Im Bank guarantee. Under limited conditions, a waiver on this condition may be granted by the Maritime Administration (MARAD).	Public Resolution 17 of the 73rd Congress; P.L. 109-304
Noncommercial or Nonfinancial Considerations	The Bank should deny applications for credit on the basis of nonfinancial and noncommercial considerations only in cases where the President, in consultation with the House Financial Services Committee and Senate Banking, Housing and Urban Affairs Committee, determines that the denial of such applications would advance U.S. national interests in areas such as international terrorism, nuclear proliferation, environmental protection, and human rights. The power to make a national interest determination has been delegated to the Secretary of State.	12 U.S.C. 635(b)(1)(B)
Cofinancing	Ex-Im Bank supports financing with ECAs in other countries through "one-stop-shop" co-financing facilities, which are arrangements that allow for Ex-Im Bank to support the U.S. content of an export, while allowing a foreign ECA to support its portion of the export, thereby providing greater financial coverage for the exporter and foreign buyer through a single ECA financing package.	Ex-Im Bank policy

Requirement	Description	Statutory Basis
EXPORT FOCUS AREAS AND LIMITATIONS		
Small Businesses	Congress directs the Bank to make available not less than 20% of its aggregate loan, guarantee, and insurance authority to finance exports directly by U.S. small businesses.	12 U.S.C. 635(b)(1)(E)(v)
Renewable Energy	Congress directs the Bank to promote the export of U.S. goods and services related to renewable energy sources. Appropriations language further has specified the Bank should make available not less than 10% of its aggregate authority to finance exports of renewable energy technologies or energy efficient end-use technologies.	12 U.S.C. 635(b)(1)(K)
Sub-Saharan Africa	Congress directs the Bank to promote the expansion of its financial commitments in sub-Saharan Africa, in consultation with the Trade Promotion Coordinating Committee (TPCC). No quantitative target is specified.	12 U.S.C. 635(b)(9)(A)
Country Restrictions	The Bank generally is prohibited from extending credit and insurance to certain countries, including but not limited to those that are in armed conflict with the United States, those with balance of payment problems, or those for which a Presidential determination has been issued.	12 U.S.C. 635(b)(2)
Military Exports	Ex-Im Bank is prohibited from financing defense articles and defense services with certain limited exceptions.	12 U.S.C. 635(b)(6)(A)

Source: CRS analysis of Ex-Im Bank charter (12 U.S.C. 635 et. seq.) and policy documents.

Financial Products

Ex-Im Bank groups its financial products into four main categories: (1) direct loans; (2) loan guarantees; (3) working capital finance; and (4) export credit insurance (see **text box** at end of section for examples of transactions).[4] Its commitments and repayment periods can range from short-term (less than one year); medium-term (one to seven years); and long-term (more than seven years). The Bank may determine repayment terms based on variables such as buyer, industry, and country conditions; common repayment terms that the market gives such products; terms of international rules on export credit activity; and the matching of terms offered by foreign ECAs. Ex-Im Bank, a demand-driven agency, charges interest, risk premia, and other fees for its services.

Direct Loans

Ex-Im Bank provides direct loans to foreign buyers of U.S. goods and services, usually for U.S. capital equipment and services (see **Figure 1**). Direct loans have no minimum or maximum size, but generally involve amounts of more than $10 million. The Bank extends to the U.S. company's foreign customer a loan covering up to 85% of the U.S. contract value. Direct loans are available for medium- and long-term transactions, but most commonly are offered on a long-term basis. The direct loans carry fixed interest rates and generally are made at terms that are the most

---

[4] Information drawn from Ex-Im Bank, http://www.exim.gov/.

attractive allowed under the provisions of the OECD Arrangement. The specific rates charged by Ex-Im Bank are based on the Commercial Interest Reference Rates (CIRR).[5]

Figure 1. Ex-Im Bank Direct Loan Structure

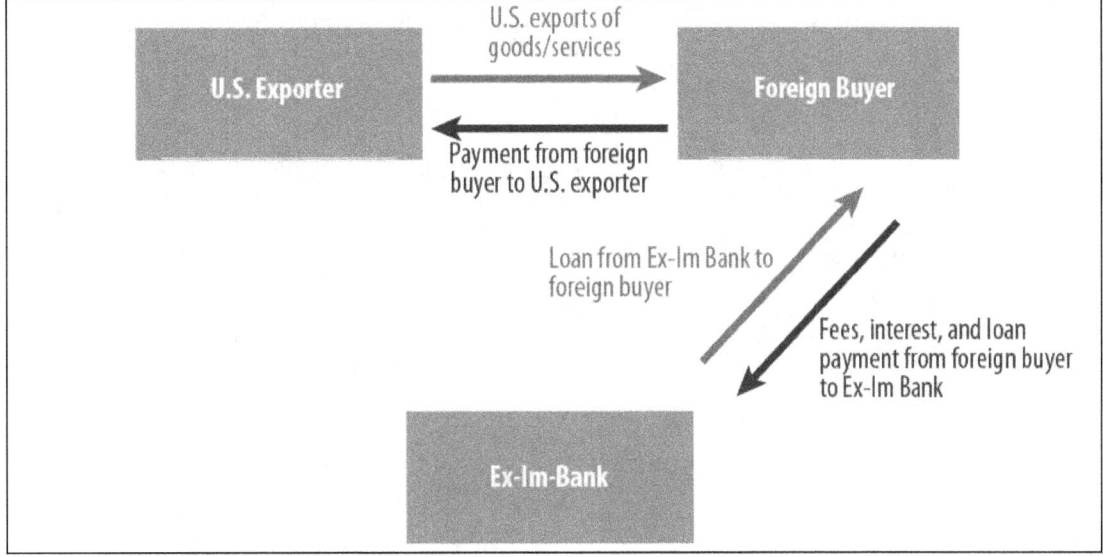

Source: CRS, based on Ex-Im Bank information.

Notes: This diagram is a general representation of Ex-Im Bank direct loans. Specifics vary by transaction.

Prior to 1980, Ex-Im Bank's direct lending program was its chief financing vehicle. Both the budget authority requested by the Administration and the level approved by Congress for direct lending dropped sharply during the 1980s, reportedly as a target of budget cuts.[6] In the past decade, demand for Ex-Im Bank direct loans has been limited, because commercial interest rates were low.[7] According to the Bank, demand for direct loans increased significantly with the international financial crisis of 2008-2009, as banking problems limited the ability of commercial banks to originate export finance transactions at competitive rates.[8]

Medium- and Long-Term Loan Guarantees

Ex-Im Bank provides medium- and long-term guarantees of loans made by a lender to a foreign buyer of U.S. goods and services, promising to pay the lender, if the buyer defaults, the

---

[5] Commercial Interest Reference Rates (CIRRs) are the official lending rates of ECAs. They are calculated monthly and based on government bonds issued in the country's domestic market for its currency. For the U.S. dollar, the CIRR is based on the U.S. Treasury bond rate. Ex-Im Bank, "Commercial Interest Reference Rates," http://www.exim.gov/ tools/commercialinterestreferencerates/index.cfm/.

[6] Ex-Im Bank, Office of the Inspector General (OIG), *Export-Import Bank's Management of Direct Loans and Related Challenges*, OIG-AR-13-05, September 26, 2013, p. 1, http://www.exim.gov/oig/upload/OIG-Final-Report-Audit-of-Ex-Im-Bank-s-Management-of-Direct-Loans-and-Related-Challenges-09-26-13-2.pdf.

[7] Ibid.

[8] Ex-Im Bank, *Report to the U.S. Congress on Export Credit Competition and the Export-Import Bank of the United States, For the Period January 1, 2012 through December 31, 2012*, Washington, DC, June 2013, p. 45, http://www.exim.gov/about/library/reports/competitivenessreports/upload/US-Ex-Im-Bank-2012-Competitiveness-Report-to-Congress-Complete.pdf (hereinafter Ex-Im Bank, *2012 Competitiveness Report*, June 2013).

---

outstanding principal and accrued interest on the loan (see **Figure 2**). Loan guarantees are intended to cover repayment risk. Medium- and long-term loan guarantees are typically used to finance purchases of U.S. capital equipment and services. Unlike insurance (discussed below), loan guarantees are *unconditional*—representing Ex-Im Bank's commitment to a commercial bank for full repayment in the event of a default. There is no limit on the transaction size for a loan guarantee. Ex-Im Bank provides a guarantee of up to 85% or 100% of the U.S. content, whichever is lower, with a minimum 15% down payment required from the buyer. It provides coverage for 100% of the commercial and political risks of borrower repayment.

Figure 2. Ex-Im Bank Loan Guarantee Structure

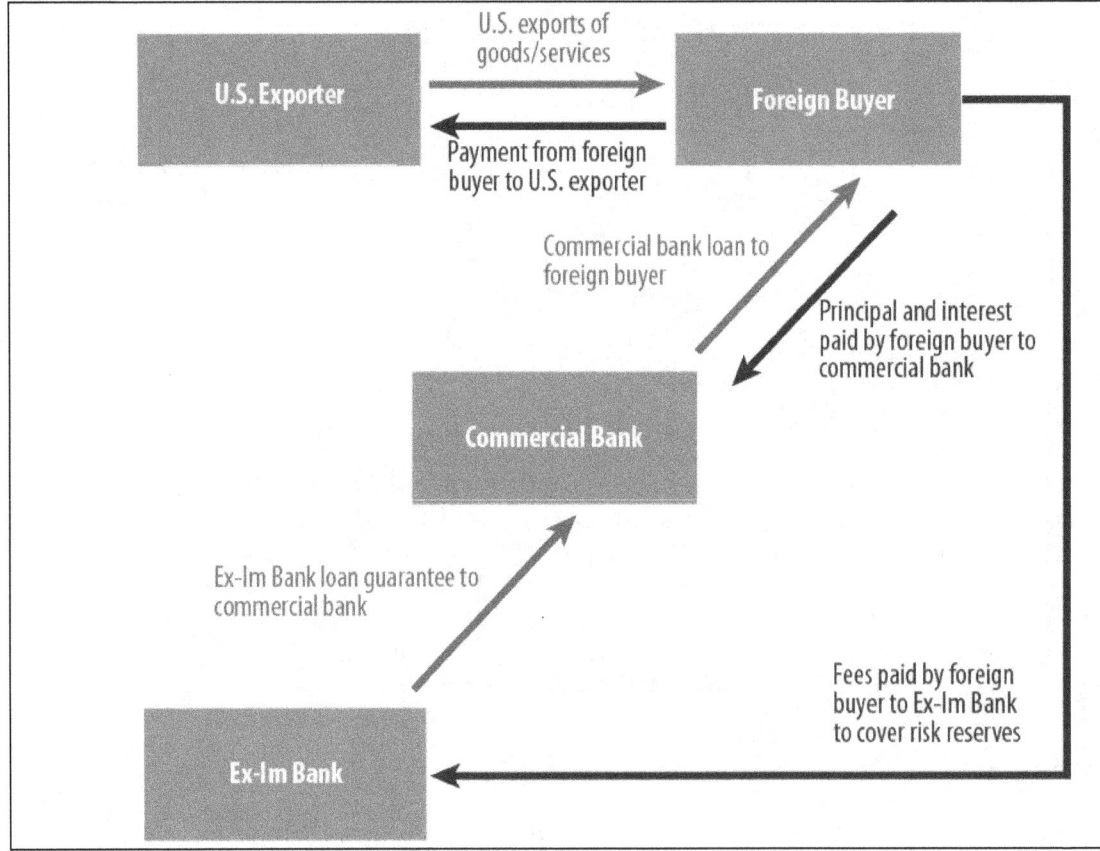

Source: CRS, based on Ex-Im Bank information.

Notes: This diagram is a general representation of Ex-Im Bank loan guarantees. Specifics vary by transaction.

Working Capital Financing

Ex-Im Bank's working capital program is intended to facilitate finance for businesses, primarily small businesses, which have exporting potential but need working capital funds (e.g., to buy raw materials or supplies) to produce or market their goods or services for export.

Working capital guarantees provide repayment guarantees to lenders (primarily commercial banks) on secured, short- and medium-term working capital loans made to qualified exporters. They can be for a single loan or a revolving line of credit, and typically are for one year, but can be extended to up to three years. Working capital guarantees cover up to 90% of the principal and interest on a loan made to an exporter by a private lender for export-related accounts receivables, and up to 75% for export-related inventory. Generally, each product must have more than 50% U.S. content based on all direct and indirect costs for eligibility. The interest rates for working capital loans guaranteed by Ex-Im Bank are set by the commercial lender. The working capital guarantees are secured by export-related accounts receivable and inventory (including work-in-process). The collateral requirement under the guaranteed loan to issue letters of credit is 25% of the face value of the letter of credit, compared with the standard 100% cash collateral generally required by the private sector. On a case-by-case basis, the letter of credit collateral requirement may be lowered to 10%. **Working capital loans** are fixed-rate lines of credit to small business exporters of up to $500,000 for a 6-month or 12-month period.

Export Credit Insurance

Ex-Im Bank provides insurance policies to exporters and lenders to protect against losses of non-repayment for commercial and political reasons. Like loan guarantees, insurance is intended to reduce the risks involved in exporting by protecting against commercial or political uncertainty. However, in contrast, insurance is *conditional* on the fulfillment of various requirements for Ex-Im Bank to pay a claim (e.g., compliance with underwriting policies, deadlines for filing claims, payment of premiums and fees, and submission of proper documentation).[9]

The Bank issues short-term insurance policies to U.S. exporters to reduce their risk of nonpayment by the foreign buyer. Insurance, for example, could allow the exporter to extend more competitive terms of credit to foreign buyers (see **Figure 3**) and/or provide additional working capital to increase the exporter's borrowing base. Short-term exporter insurance is available for products shipped from the United States and with at least 50% U.S. content (excluding mark-up). Ex-Im Bank offers a renewable one-year policy that generally covers up to 180-day terms, but can be extended up to 360 days for qualifying transactions. It also maintains short-term insurance policies for lenders. Depending on the policy, the Bank will cover 90-95% of nonpayment losses due to commercial and political risks.

---

[9] U.S. Government Accountability Office (GAO), *Export-Import Bank: Recent Growth Underscores Need for Continued Improvements in Risk Management*, GAO-13-303, March 2013, p. 41, http://www.gao.gov/products/GAO-13-303.

Figure 3. Ex-Im Bank Exporter Insurance Structure

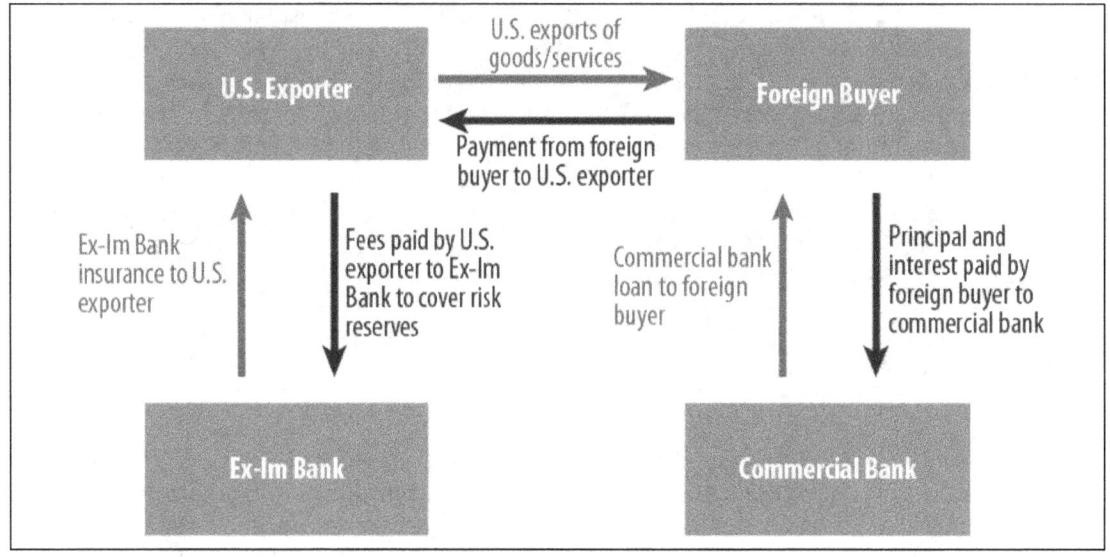

Source: CRS, based on Ex-Im Bank information.

Notes: This diagram is a general representation of Ex-Im Bank exporter insurance. Specifics vary by transaction.

Ex-Im Bank can extend medium-term insurance, generally up to five years and with a maximum cover of $10 million, to both exporters and lenders, covering one or a series of shipments. The Bank will insure up to 85% of the contract price prior to delivery. If the foreign content is more than 15%, it will only support the U.S. portion. It requires the buyer to make cash payment to the exporter equal to 15% of the net U.S. contract value. It covers 100% of nonpayment due to commercial and political risk.

Specialized Finance Products

Ex-Im Bank's programs include specialized finance products[10], such as:

- **project finance,** which is limited recourse project finance to newly created companies, usually in amounts greater than $10 million. Project finance typically covers large, long-term infrastructure and industrial projects (e.g., airport construction, oil and gas power sector projects, wind turbines), involving multiple contracts for completion and operation. Sponsor support during construction, combined with the project's future cash flows, form the basis for the Bank's analysis of the creditworthiness of the project, as well as its source of repayment (rather than repayments by foreign governments, financial institutions, or established corporations). Repayment terms are generally up to 14 years, but can be up to 18 years for renewable energy projects.

- **structured finance,** which is finance to existing companies located overseas, based on their balance sheets and other sources of collateral or security enhancements. Through structured finance, Ex-Im Bank has financed fiber-optic

---

[10] The specialized finance products summarized in this section are classified under Ex-Im Bank's loan guarantee program on the agency's website (http://www.exim.gov/), but may include direct loan and/or insurance support as well.

cable, oil and gas projects, air traffic control systems, satellites, and manufacturing equipment. Repayment terms generally are for up to 10 years, but can be up to 12 years for power transactions.

- **transportation finance**, including for aircraft, ship, and railroad exports, based on the guidelines set by specific sector understanding under the OECD Arrangement.

Examples of Ex-Im Bank Transactions

Direct Loans

In May 2012, Ex-Im Bank provided a $48.6 million direct loan to Gas Verde, S.A. for a biogas project in Brazil for the export of U.S. renewable energy technologies from FirmGreen, a small U.S. business based in California, and other U.S. suppliers.

In January 2013, Ex-Im Bank authorized a $155.4 million direct loan to Ghana to finance the design and construction of a hospital expansion, which will support U.S. exports of engineering and construction services and medical appliances by Americaribe Inc. (Miami, FL).

In September 2013, Ex-Im Bank authorized two direct loans totaling $33.6 million to Abengoa, a Spanish multinational company, to support the export of U.S. heat-transfer fluid produced by The Dow Chemical Company for use in solar projects in Spain and South Africa.

Loan Guarantees

In March 2013, Ex-Im Bank approved a final commitment of a $1.1 billion loan guarantee to finance the export of a fleet of Boeing aircraft to Lion Air, a privately-owned airline in Indonesia. Apple Bank for Savings (New York) provided the financing, with the possibility of additional funding provided by capital market investors through an Ex-Im Bank-guaranteed bond.

In June 2013, Ex-Im Bank authorized a $19.9 million loan guarantee extended by HSBC Bank to a Nigerian company to facilitate the export of one used liftboat provided by Offshore Liftboats LLC, a U.S. small business based in Louisiana.

Export Credit Insurance

In September 2012, Ex-Im Bank authorized $900,000 in export credit insurance to support the export of agricultural aircraft by Air Tractor Inc. to Brazil.

Project Finance Direct Loan

In December 2013, Ex-Im Bank authorized a $694.4 million loan to Roy Hill Holdings (Australia) contingent on the purchase U.S. mining and rail equipment from Caterpillar Inc., General Electric, and Atlas Copco. Ex-Im Bank financing was part of a $7.2 billion long-term financing agreement to fund a $10 billion, 55-million metric tons per year iron ore mining project by Roy Hill. The financing agreement consists of loans and guarantees from five export credit agencies from the United States, Japan, and South Korea and a consortium of 19 commercial banks from Australia, Japan, Europe, China, Korea and Singapore.

Source: Various Ex-Im Bank and other press releases.

Activity Level

Focus Areas

While Ex-Im Bank is a demand-driven agency, it has certain focus areas. As previously discussed, Congress requires Ex-Im Bank to support certain types of exports, that is, exports by U.S. small businesses, U.S. renewable energy exports, and U.S. exports to sub-Saharan Africa. The Bank also seeks to support U.S. exports based on Administration goals and policy initiatives. For example, under the Obama Administration, Ex-Im Bank has been involved in efforts to boost U.S.

exports worldwide under the National Export Initiative, as well as regional initiatives focused on sub-Saharan Africa and the Asia-Pacific region. Key focus areas for the Bank include the following.

- **Geographical focus:** The Bank is open to support buyers of U.S. exports in 175 countries around the world. Congress has identified sub-Saharan Africa as a priority region. Countries subject to U.S. sanctions are ineligible for Ex-Im Bank support, as well as certain other countries under the charter's current Marxist-Leninist prohibition.

- **Sectoral focus:** Ex-Im Bank has identified several industries with high potential for U.S. export growth: oil and gas, mining, agribusiness, renewable energy, medical equipment and services, construction equipment and services, aircraft, and power generation and related services. Infrastructure development is a major focus of the Bank's financing. Military or defense items, as well as sales to military buyers, generally are ineligible for support, with certain exceptions.

- **Focus on specific types of exporters:** Ex-Im Bank has a long-standing focus on supporting exports of U.S. small- and medium-sized enterprises (SMEs).

Authorizations

In FY2013, Ex-Im Bank approved 3,842 transactions of credit and insurance support, which amounted to $27.3 billion in approved commitments. U.S. small businesses account for the majority of Ex-Im Bank's transactions by *number* (89% in FY2013), while larger companies represent the majority by *dollar amount*. Ex-Im Bank reported that 42% of its total authorizations for FY2013 supported infrastructure projects.[11] The *number* of transactions authorized in FY2013 reached a record high. However, in terms of authorization *value*, after several years of record highs, the amount authorized in FY2013 declined (see **Figure 4**). The dynamics could reflect recovery of the financial markets in some areas; increased focus on supporting small business export transactions (high in number, but of lower value than larger transactions); and the absence of certain large transactions in certain markets, such as for aircraft.

---

[11] Ex-Im Bank, *FY2013 Annual Report*, p. 4.

Figure 4. Ex-Im Bank Authorizations, FY1997-FY2013

Billions of U.S. Dollars

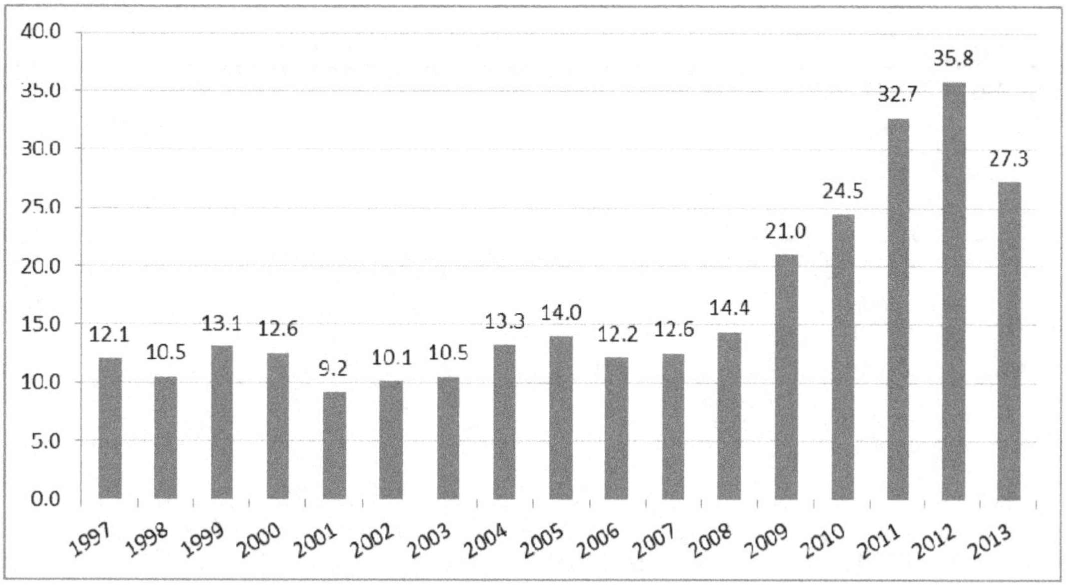

Source: CRS, from Ex-Im Bank annual reports.

Ex-Im Bank has met its small business mandate from Congress in some years, but has fallen short in other years (see **Table 2**). At the same time, the number of small business transactions supported by the Bank continues to increase. For environmentally beneficial exports, the Bank has been consistently well below the 10% target, closer to 2%, possibly due, in part, to limitations in the U.S. supply of renewable energy exports.[12] Nevertheless, the Bank's authorization amounts for renewable energy exports have increased. Ex-Im Bank's support for sub-Saharan Africa also reflects an overall uptick in activity, compared to previous years. While the Bank seeks to support these export goals, its actual activity depends on alignment with commercial interests as it is demand-driven.

---

[12] GAO, *Export-Import Bank: Reaching New Targets for Environmentally Beneficial Exports Presents Major Challenges for Bank*, GAO-10-682, July 14, 2010, http://www.gao.gov/products/GAO-10-682.

Table 2. Ex-Im Bank's Credit and Insurance Authorizations, FY2012-FY2013

Program	Number of Authorizations		Amount Authorized ($ millions)	
	2012	2013	2012	2013
Total Authorizations	**3,796**	**3,842**	**$35,784**	**$27,347**
Loans	24	71	$11,765.7	$6,893.8
Loan Guarantees	744	674	$18,319.3	$14,911.8
Insurance	3,028	3,097	$5,699.3	$5,542.0
Authorizations for Specific Types of Exports (Congressional Mandate)				
Exports by Small Business (20% target for amount)	3,313	3,413	$6,123	$5,223
Percent of Total	87.3%	88.8%	17.1%	19.1%
Environmentally Beneficial Exports (10% target for amount)	149	143	$615	$433
Percent of Total	3.9%	3.7%	1.7%	1.6%
Exports to Sub-Saharan Africa (increased focus, no % target)	163	188	$1,522	$604
Percent of Total	4.3%	4.9%	4.3%	2.2%

Source: Ex-Im Bank Annual Reports data adapted by CRS.

Ex-Im Bank estimates that its FY2013 authorizations supported $37.4 billion in U.S. exports of goods and services and 205,000 U.S. jobs.[13] Ex-Im Bank finances around 2% of U.S. exports annually, but possibly a higher percentage for certain sectors of the U.S. economy.

Portfolio Exposure

Congress sets limitations in Ex-Im Bank's charter on the aggregate amounts of loan, guarantees, and insurance that the Bank can have outstanding at any one time (oftentimes referred to as the Bank's exposure cap/ceiling/limit).[14] The outstanding principal amount of all loans made, guaranteed, or insured by Ex-Im Bank is charged at the full value against the limitation.

In FY2013, the Bank reported a total portfolio exposure of $113.8 billion—below the $130 billion statutory cap for that year. Its portfolio is distributed across its financial products, as well as geographical regions and economic sectors (see **Figure 5**). Ex-Im Bank's exposure level has been at record highs in recent years (see **Figure 6**), associated largely with increased demand for Ex-Im Bank's services during the financial crisis as commercial lending declined. Other possible drivers could be greater demand in emerging markets for U.S. exports; increased usage of the Bank by key customers, such as those in the satellite sector; and greater Ex-Im Bank outreach to small businesses and exporters in key markets.[15] For FY2014, the Bank's statutory exposure limit is $140 billion.

---

[13] Ibid., p. 5.

[14] 12 U.S.C §635e.

[15] GAO, *Export-Import Bank: Recent Growth Underscores Need for Continued Improvements in Risk Management*, GAO-13-303, March 2013, pp. 14-20.

Figure 5. Ex-Im Bank Exposure Level by Program, Geographic Region, and Economic Sector, FY2013

Billions of U.S. Dollars

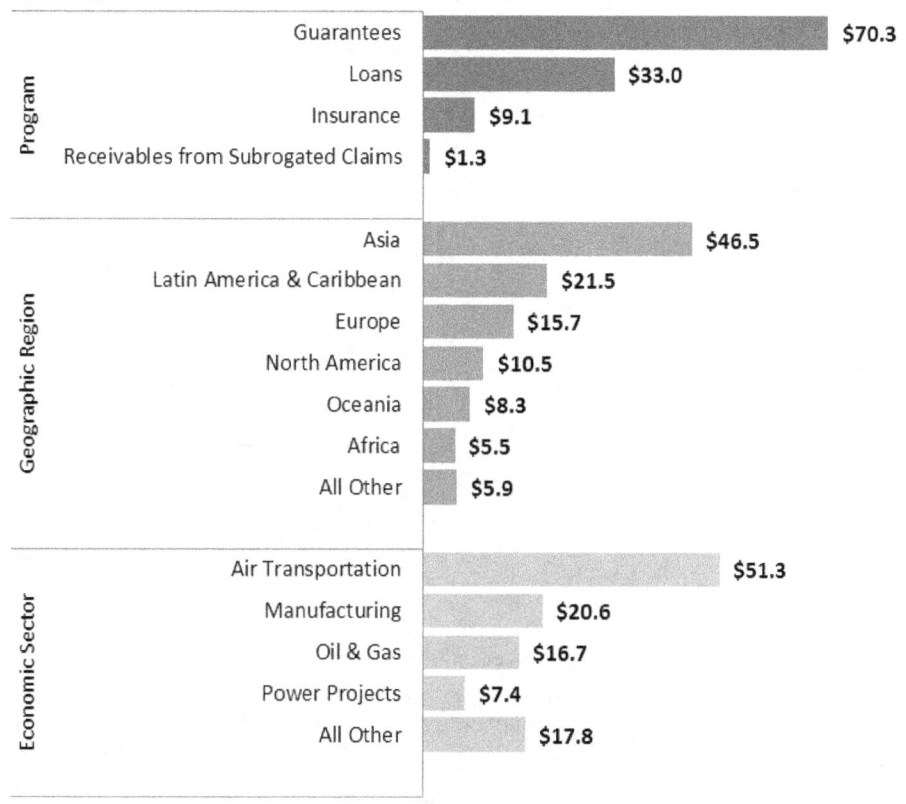

Ex-Im Bank reported its FY2013 exposure as $113.8 billion

Program
- Guarantees: $70.3
- Loans: $33.0
- Insurance: $9.1
- Receivables from Subrogated Claims: $1.3

Geographic Region
- Asia: $46.5
- Latin America & Caribbean: $21.5
- Europe: $15.7
- North America: $10.5
- Oceania: $8.3
- Africa: $5.5
- All Other: $5.9

Economic Sector
- Air Transportation: $51.3
- Manufacturing: $20.6
- Oil & Gas: $16.7
- Power Projects: $7.4
- All Other: $17.8

Source: CRS, based on data from Ex-Im Bank annual reports.

Figure 6. Ex-Im Bank Exposure Levels and Exposure Cap, FY1997-FY2013

Billions of U.S. Dollars

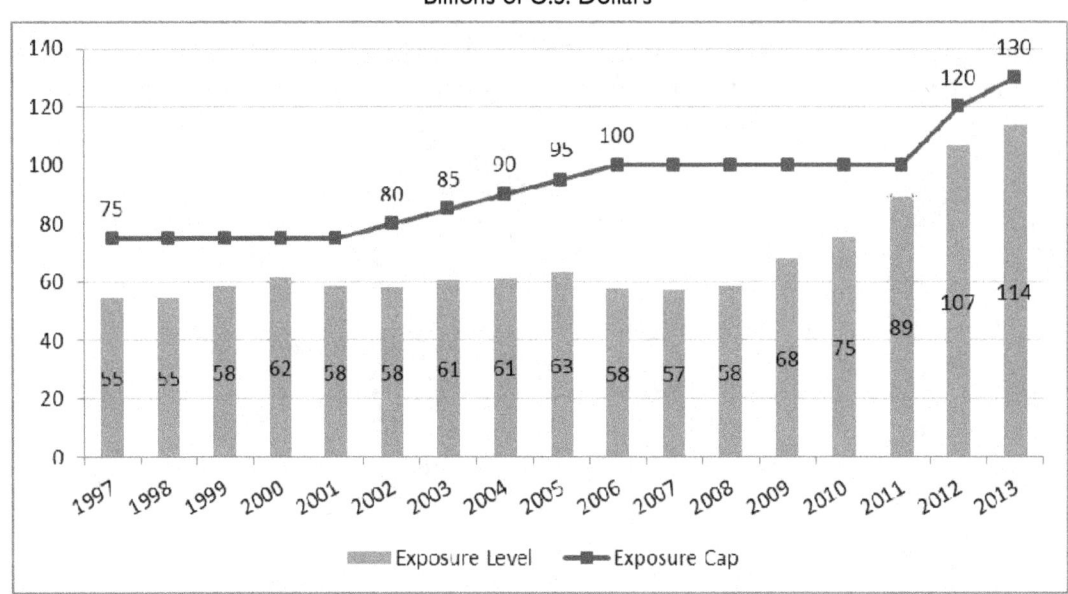

Source: CRS analysis of data from Ex-Im Bank annual reports.

Ex-Im Bank Budget

Beginning with FY1992, Ex-Im Bank's operations have been subject to the Federal Credit Reform Act of 1990 (FCRA, P.L. 101-508), which was intended to measure more accurately the cost of federal credit programs and to make the cost of such credit programs more comparable to direct federal outlays.[16] For a given fiscal year, under FCRA, the cost of federal credit activities, including those of Ex-Im Bank, is reported on an *accrual basis* equivalent with other federal spending, rather than on a *cash flow basis*, as used previously. Under FCRA's rules, budget estimates are calculated by discounting them using the rates on U.S. Treasury securities with similar terms to maturity—which traditionally have been considered to be risk-free—and are below the rates of commercial loans. The Bank's estimates now allocate budgetary resources to reserve against its estimated risk of loss.[17]

Between 1992 and 2008, the Bank received direct appropriations for its administrative expenses and credit subsidy. Since 2008, Congress has recognized Ex-Im Bank as a "self-sustaining" agency with a "net appropriations of zero" for appropriations purposes. In 2008, Congress gave the Bank permission to use its offsetting collections (e.g., interest, premia, and other fees charged for activities) to fund its administrative and program expenses and to retain its carryover negative subsidy ("profit") for a certain amount of time. Since then, for each year, the President has requested, and Congress has approved, that offsetting collections would count against the appropriation of operating expenses from the General Fund and that the net appropriation is

---

[16] Ex-Im Bank, *FY2013 Annual Report*.

[17] Presently, there is a debate about whether the cost of federal credit is appropriately priced under the Federal Credit Reform Act (FCRA), or if fair value accounting (discussed in the "Selected Issues for Congress" section) is a more appropriate measure. For more information, see Deborah Lucas and Marvin Phaup, "Reforming Credit Reform," *Public Budgeting & Finance*, Winter 2008.

expected to be $0. As part of the annual appropriations process, Congress sets an upper limit on the level available to the Bank for operations and provides a direct appropriation for its Office of Inspector General (OIG).

At the start of the fiscal year, the U.S. Treasury provides Ex-Im Bank with an "appropriation warrant" for program costs and administrative expenses. The amount of the warrant is established by the spending limits set by Congress in the appropriations process. The Bank retains the fees that it collects during the year that are in excess of expected losses, and uses these offsetting collections to repay the warrant, resulting in an expected net appropriation of $0. Thus, Ex-Im Bank can receive funds from the U.S. Treasury and repay those funds as offsetting collections come in.

Borrowings from the U.S. Treasury are used to finance medium- and long-term loans, and carry a fixed interest rate. Ex-Im Bank repays these borrowings primarily with the repayments of medium- and long-term loans.[18]

For FY2014, Congress set a limit of $115.5 million for Ex-Im Bank's administrative expenses and provided $5.1 million for its OIG (see **Table 3**). Congress did not appropriate any program funds, as the Bank forecasted that all new authorizations will be either zero or negative subsidy for FY2014, and did not request any positive subsidy for its program expenses.[19] Congress also allowed carryover funds of up to $10 million to remain available until September 30, 2017.

---

[18] The charter limits the aggregate amount of Ex-Im Bank's obligations outstanding (e.g., notes, debentures, and bonds) from the U.S. Treasury to $6 billion at any one time. FCRA has introduced changes to the Bank's funding process, and the Bank has proposed eliminating the corresponding language in its charter.

[19] Subsidy refers to program activities (the cost of direct loans, loan guarantees, insurance, and tied aid) conducted by Ex-Im Bank.

Table 3. Budget of the Export-Import Bank, FY2011-FY2015

Millions of U.S. Dollars

Category	FY2011	FY2012	FY2013	FY2014 Est.	FY2015 Req.
Appropriations					
Inspector General Amount Requested	3	4	4.4	5.1	5.75
Inspector General Amount Appropriated	2.5	4	4	5.1	—
Total Subsidy Requested	93	76	38	—	—
Total Subsidy Appropriated	58	58	58	—	—
Total Administrative Budget Requested	106	125	104	114.9	115.5
Total Administrative Budget Appropriated	84	90	90	115.5ᵃ	—
Total Budgetary Resources Available	1,829	1,572	1,455	1,820	356
Budget Authority (net)	443	393	624	1,412	—
Outlays (net)	158	713	939	1,491	14

Source: Office of Management and Budget, *Budget of the United States Government*, various issues.

Note: Subsidy refers to program activities (the cost of direct loans, loan guarantees, insurance, and tied aid) conducted by Ex-Im Bank. Reestimates of subsidy costs refer to reestimates of direct loan and loan guarantee subsidies and the interest on those reestimates. For FY2014 and FY2015, Ex-Im Bank forecasted that all new authorizations will be zero or negative subsidy, and did not request any positive subsidy for program expenses.

a. This amount includes a one-time appropriation of $10.5 million for the Bank's renovation expenses to its headquarters.

For FY2015, the President requested a limit of $115.5 million for Ex-Im Bank's administrative expenses and funding of $5.75 million for its OIG. The President also requested that Ex-Im Bank be allowed carryover funds of up to $10 million to remain available until September 30, 2018. The President's budget request estimates that the Bank's export credit support will total $37.6 billion, and will be funded entirely by receipts collected from the Bank's customers. The Bank estimates it will collect $1.2 billion in 2015 in receipts in excess of expected losses on transactions authorized in 2015 and prior years.

Ex-Im Bank regularly contributes to the U.S. Treasury. In FY2013, Ex-Im Bank transferred $1.1 billion to the Treasury's General Fund after covering operating expenses and loan loss reserves.

Risk Management

Ex-Im Bank seeks to manage the risks it faces in its transactions (see **Table 4**). The basis for its risk management function is in the Bank's charter, which requires that all transactions supported by the Bank have a reasonable assurance of repayment and that the Bank maintains reasonable provisions for losses. The Bank has a system in place to mitigate risks through credit underwriting and due diligence of potential transactions, as well as monitoring risks of current transactions. If a transaction has credit weaknesses, the Bank will try to restructure it to help prevent defaults and increase the likelihood of higher recoveries if the transaction does default. Ex-Im Bank also has a claims and recovery process for transactions in default.

Ex-Im Bank's reserves for loan losses total more than $4 billion. In recent years, the Bank's default rate has been less than 1%, and historically, it has been less than 2%.[20] The Bank's default rate as of March 31, 2014, was 0.211%.[21] According to a non-partisan Government Accountability Office (GAO) study, the ultimate impact of Ex-Im Bank's recent business on default rates is not yet known as it contains a large volume of transactions that have not reached their peak default periods.[22] GAO also has stated that trends in Ex-Im Bank's default rate should be viewed with caution because of limitations in the agency's analysis of its financial performance.[23]

Since 1992, Ex-Im Bank has been able to recover 50 cents on the dollar on average for transactions in default.[24] Backed by the U.S. government, Ex-Im Bank can take legal action against obligors for transactions in default. It is also able to recover assets because its loans are heavily collateralized, as a high percentage of its transactions are asset-backed (e.g., aircraft).

Table 4. Selected Risks Faced by Ex-Im Bank

Risk	Definition
Repayment	The risk that a borrower will not pay according to the original agreement and the Bank may eventually have to write-off some or all of the obligation because of credit or political reasons.
Concentration	Risk stemming from the composition of the credit portfolio as opposed to the risks related to specific obligors. Ex-Im Bank faces concentration risks in terms of the composition of its portfolio by geographic region, industry, and obligor.
Foreign Currency	Risk stemming from an appreciation or depreciation in the value of a foreign currency in relation to the U.S. dollar in Ex-Im Bank transactions denominated in that foreign currency.
Operational	The risk of material losses resulting from human error, system deficiencies, and control weaknesses.
Interest Rate	Ex-Im Bank makes fixed-rate loan commitments prior to borrowing to fund loans and takes the risk that it will have to borrow funds at an interest rate greater than the rate charged on the credit.

Source: CRS, based on Ex-Im Bank annual reports.

Ex-Im Bank in an International Context

As international trade has grown, trade finance has expanded. Some 80-90% of world trade relies on trade finance, and the global market for trade finance is estimated to be at around $10 trillion a year.[25] In addition to financing through government-backed ECAs, the private sector also

---

[20] Ex-Im Bank calculates its default rate as a "total amount of required payments that are overdue (claims paid on guarantees and insurance transactions plus loans past due) divided by a total amount of financing involved (disbursements)." Ex-Im Bank, *FY2013 Annual Report*, p. 48.

[21] CRS electronic communication with Ex-Im Bank, May 30, 2014.

[22] GAO, *Export-Import Bank: Recent Growth Underscores Need for Continued Improvements in Risk Management*, GAO-13-303, March 2013, p. 31.

[23] GAO, *Export-Import Bank: Recent Growth Underscores Need for Continued Improvements in Risk Management*, GAO-13-703T, June 13, 2013, p. 6.

[24] Ex-Im Bank, *FY2013 Annual Report*.

[25] World Trade Organization, "Trade Finance: The Challenges of Trade Financing," http://www.wto.org/english/ thewto_e/coher_e/challenges_e htm.

provides export financing, including through commercial backs, capital markets, lessors, and manufacturing self-financing. While the private sector is the leading source of export finance, ECAs are considered in the trade finance community to play an important role in certain niches. Most developed countries and many developing countries have ECAs. Outside of the United States, upwards of 60 ECAs exist in foreign countries.

The relative attractiveness of seeking export financing through the private sector, ECAs, or a combination of both can change depending on credit market conditions in the private sector, as well as how ECA financing terms may change or respond to these market conditions. In recent years, the role of ECAs may have become more prominent, in part, due to tight credit market conditions associated with the international financial crisis and the regulatory impact of Basel III on commercial banks.[26] Private lenders and insurers conduct the majority of short-term export financing, though ECAs may play an active role in supporting certain sectors, such as taking on risks of financing small business exports. ECAs also appear to be more heavily involved in longer-term export financing, including financing for complex, multi-billion dollar sales such as aircraft and infrastructure projects. In such sectors, the private sector plays an active role, but in certain cases, ECA support can help make transactions more commercially attractive by mitigating risks of financing or by providing an additional source of funding to diversify risks of financing.

International Rules on Official Export Credit Activity

The Organization for Economic Cooperation and Development (OECD) Arrangement on Officially Supported Export Credits (the "OECD Arrangement") guides the scope of certain financing activities of Ex-Im Bank and other participating foreign ECAs (generally developed countries).[27] The United States generally opposes subsidies for exports of commercial products. Since the 1970s, the United States has led efforts within the OECD to adopt international protocols which reduce the subsidy level in export credits by raising the interest rates on government-provided export credits to reflect market levels more closely.

The OECD Arrangement, which came into effect in April 1978, establishes minimum interest rates and premiums, maximum repayment terms, guidelines for classifying risk, and other terms and conditions for government-backed export financing. The Arrangement has been revised a number of times over the years. For example, participants agreed to tighten restrictions on the use of tied aid (see **text box**).[28] In addition, sector understandings govern the terms and conditions of exports of, for example, civilian aircraft, ships, nuclear power plants, renewable energy, and railway infrastructure.

---

[26] Ex-Im Bank, Report to the U.S. Congress on Export Credit Competition and the Export-Import Bank of the United States, For the Period January 1, 2013 through December 31, 2013, June 2014, pp. 12-14, http://www.exim.gov/about/library/reports/competitivenessreports/upload/Ex-Im-Bank-2013-Competitiveness-Report-to-Congress-Complete.pdf (hereinafter Ex-Im Bank, 2013 Competitiveness Report, June 2014). For more information, see CRS Report R42744, U.S. Implementation of the Basel Capital Regulatory Framework, by Darryl E. Getter.

[27] For more information, see CRS Report RS21128, *The Organization for Economic Cooperation and Development*, by James K. Jackson.

[28] According to Ex-Im Bank, tied aid is a "concessional, trade-related aid credit provided by a donor government to induce the borrower to purchase equipment from suppliers in a donor's country," and "can distort trade flows when the recipient country makes its purchasing decisions on the bidder offering the cheapest financing rather than the best price, quality or service." Ex-Im Bank, *2013 Competitiveness Report*, June 2014, p. 69.

Tied Aid

Ex-Im Bank has a Tied Aid Capital Projects Fund (TACPF), often referred to as the tied aid "war chest," to counter specific projects that are receiving foreign officially-subsidized export financing. The 1986 Ex-Im Bank reauthorization act (P.L. 99-472) required the Bank to establish the tied aid fund. The Bank may conduct tied aid transactions to counter attempts by foreign governments to sway purchases in favor of their exporters solely on the basis of subsidized financing, rather than on market conditions (price, quality, etc.). The United States ties substantial amounts of its agricultural and military aid to purchases of U.S. goods, but generally has avoided using such financing to promote American capital goods exports.

The amount of funds in the TACPF was $179 million at the end of 2013. Funds for the tied aid war chest are available to the Bank. Applications for the tied aid fund are subject to review by the Treasury Department. Between 2008 and 2012, Ex-Im Bank approved two tied aid transactions, one for a waste water treatment plant in sub-Saharan Africa in 2010 and the other for the sale of fire trucks to Indonesia in 2011.

Ex-Im Bank abides by the "Helsinki Disciplines," which are rules on tied aid agreed to by OECD Arrangement participants and include notification requirements for tied aid activity. In 2013, there were 109 Helsinki-type tied aid notifications totaling approximately $4.4 billion.

Source: Ex-Im Bank, *2013 Competitiveness Report*, June 2014, pp. 73 and 75.

OECD member countries also have agreed to other guidelines for official export credit. For example, in 2007, members agreed to revise guidelines on environmental procedures, referred to as "Common Approaches on Environment and Officially Supported Export Credits." These environmental guidelines call for member governments to review projects for potential environmental impacts; to assess them against international standards, such as those of the World Bank; and to provide more public disclosure for environmentally-sensitive projects. The OECD also adopted new guidelines on sustainable lending principles that aim to help developing countries avoid a renewed build-up of debt after receiving debt relief, as well as an anti-bribery agreement.

Export credit financing that is covered by the OECD Arrangement generally is exempt from the World Trade Organization (WTO) Agreement on Subsidies and Countervailing Measures (SCM), which disciplines the use of export subsidies and the actions countries can take to counter the effects of these subsidies. The SCM Agreement is interpreted to indicate that, for non-agricultural products, an export credit practice in conformity with the OECD Arrangement on export credits shall not be considered as an export subsidy prohibited by the SCM Agreement.[29]

Growth in Unregulated Financing

The OECD Arrangement does not cover all officially supported export credit activity. According to Ex-Im Bank, in 2013, traditional OECD export financing support represented 34% of total government-backed trade-related support (see **Figure 7**).[30] Sources of government-backed export financing support that are unregulated by the OECD Arrangement are (1) emerging economies that are not a part of the OECD providing export financing through their ECAs; and (2) OECD members providing forms of export financing that are not regulated by the OECD Arrangement.

---

[29] The relationship between the OECD Arrangement and the SCM Agreement is established by Section (k) of Annex I to the SCM. See http://www.wto.org/english/res_e/booksp_e/analytic_index_e/subsidies_05_e htm.

[30] Ex-Im Bank, *2013 Competitiveness Report*, June 2014, pp. 20-21.

Figure 7. Global Government-Backed Export Support, 2013

Billions of U.S. Dollars

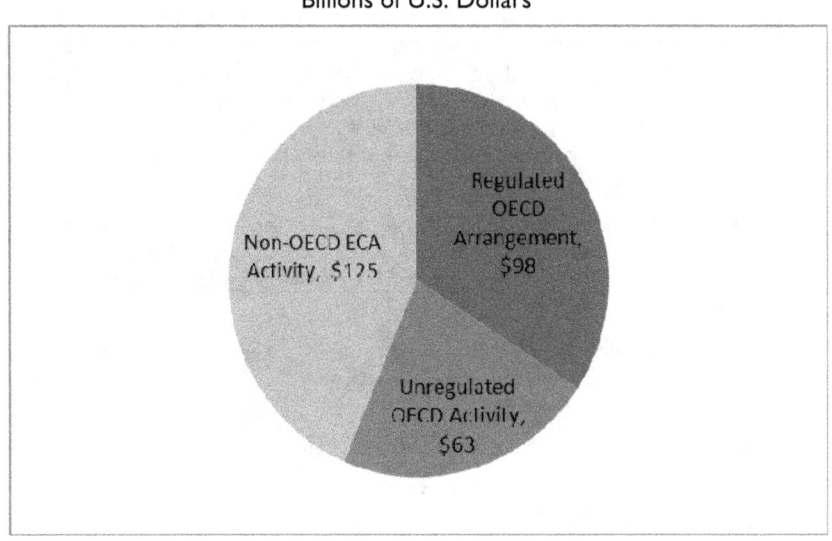

Source: Ex-Im Bank, *Report to the U.S. Congress on Export Credit Competition and the Export-Import Bank of the United States, For the Period January 1, 2013 through December 31, 2013,* June 2014, pp. 20-21.

Emerging markets such as China, Brazil, and India are not members of the OECD, but are increasingly active providers of government-backed export credit financing.[31] In 2013, new medium- and long-term government-backed export financing conducted by the 34 members of the OECD as a whole stood at $97.9 billion, down about 22% from 2012 (see **Figure 8**; see **Appendix** for expanded data). U.S. new medium- and long-term support totaled $14.5 billion in 2013. In contrast, the combined new medium- and long-term financing provided by China, Brazil, and India was $55.4 billion, up a little over 10% from 2013. Notably, China alone accounted for at least $45 billion of new official medium- and long-term export credit financing in 2013.[32]

---

[31] These emerging markets, while not members of the OECD, may have observer status during some OECD meetings. The OECD has offered them "enhanced engagement" with a view towards possible accession. Brazil, furthermore, is a member of the OECD Aircraft Sector Understanding.

[32] Ex-Im Bank, *2013 Competitiveness Report*, Washington, DC, June 2014.

Figure 8. New Medium- and Long-Term Official Export Financing Volumes for Selected ECAs, 2013

Billions of U.S. Dollars

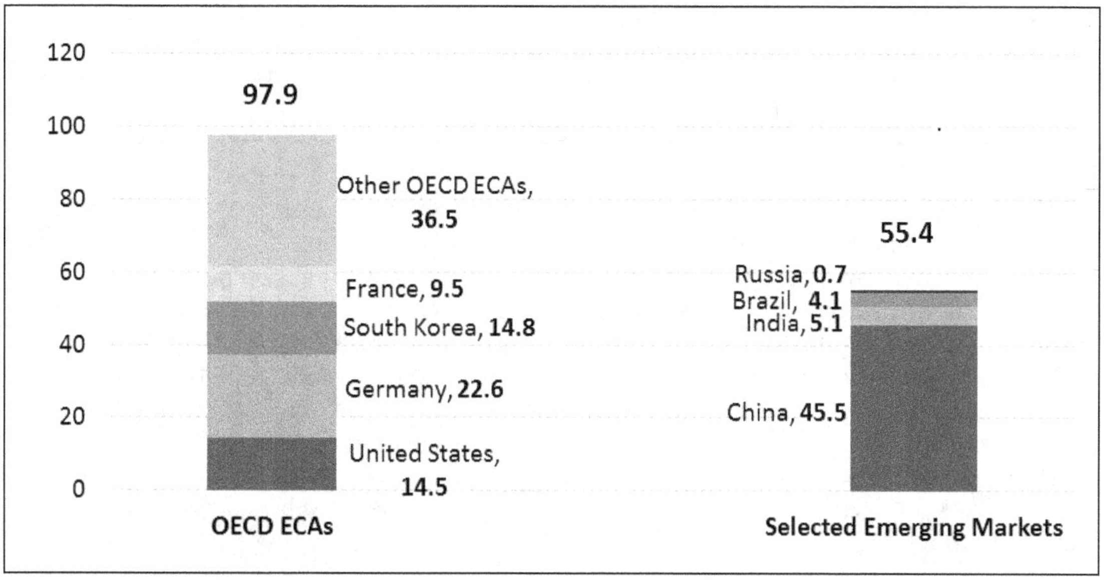

Source: Ex-Im Bank, *Report to the U.S. Congress on Export Credit Competition and the Export-Import Bank of the United States, For the Period January 1, 2013 through December 31, 2013,* June 2014.

Notes: The OECD amount totaled $119.6 billion, and the emerging market amount totaled $58.3 billion. Data subject to analytic assumptions and limited by availability of information.

The government-backed export credit activities of these non-OECD countries may not comply with international export credit standards.[11] China, Brazil, and India may offer below-market and concessionary financing alternatives with which it is difficult for ECAs of OECD members to compete (see **text box**). For example, in 2011, Brazil's largest landline telephone company reportedly chose to purchase network equipment from China's Huawei Technologies because of access to China Development Bank's $30 billion credit line, a two-year grace period on payments, and an interest rate of two percentage points below the London interbank offered rate (LIBOR).[33] Officially-backed export credit activity by emerging economies may increase in strategic markets, such as oil and gas, renewable energy, and natural resources extraction. For instance, Chinese ECAs "have shown strong signs of growing usage of export credits for export promotion purposes, especially in Africa, where they were offering preferential loans either in exchange for much needed resources (e.g., oil) or low cost loans on very extended repayment terms on projects in order to gain market share."[34]

---

[33] Gary Clyde Hufbauer, Meera Fickling, and Woan Foong Wong, *Revitalizing the Export-Import Bank,* Peterson Institute for International Economics (IIE), Number PB11-6, May 2011, http://www.iie.com/publications/pb/pb11-06.pdf. "Huawei's $30 Billion China Credit Opens Doors in Brazil, Mexico," *Bloomberg,* April 24, 2011.

[34] Ex-Im Bank, *Report to the U.S. Congress on Export Credit Competition and the Export-Import Bank of the United States, For the Period January 1, 2009 through December 31, 2009,* Washington, DC, June 2010.

Comparison of Repayment Terms for Rail Exports

The new OECD Rail Sector Understanding, concluded in September 2013, sets guidelines for railway infrastructure exports. It provides repayment terms up to 12 years for transactions in high-income OECD countries, subject to conditions aimed at complementing the private sector, and up to 14 years for transactions in all other countries. The guidelines are applicable to a market expected to exceed $120 billion annually over the 2015-2017 period.[35] In contrast to OECD repayment terms, various studies suggest that China's repayment terms for its rail exports, such as for infrastructure projects in sub-Saharan Africa, can exceed 20 years.[36]

The ECAs of OECD member countries also conduct export credit financing and other activities that fall outside of the Arrangement. One form of unregulated financing is the "market window," which is a government-owned entity or program that offers export credits on market terms. Market windows generally do not operate on purely commercial terms, as they tend to receive benefits from their government status that commercial lenders cannot access. Many ECAs operate market windows, such as Canada, Germany, and Italy; Ex-Im Bank does not have a market window. It is difficult to obtain data on market window operations of foreign countries. Another form of unregulated financing is untied lending support, which is credit support extended by a government entity to a recipient for the purpose of providing credit for strategic interests of the donor country. Because the untied loan is not tied to exports, it is not subject to the OECD export credit guidelines.

Developments in International Export Credit Negotiations

As stated previously, the United States historically has led efforts to impose international disciplines on government-backed export credit activity. The 2012 Ex-Im Bank reauthorization act went further, directing the Secretary of the Treasury (which takes the lead on U.S. international export credit negotiations) to negotiate to reduce and eliminate government-backed ECA financing altogether. Congress also required the Secretary of the Treasury to negotiate with all countries that finance air carrier aircraft through funds from a state-sponsored entity to reduce and eliminate aircraft export credit financing for all aircraft covered by the 2007 OECD Aircraft Sector Understanding. These efforts reportedly have run into difficulty in the OECD. While exports play an important role in the U.S. economy, the economies of other countries are far more reliant on exports, constituting a larger share of their respective gross domestic product (GDP). Moreover, other OECD countries presumably would be reluctant to terminate their export credit programs while countries outside of the OECD, such as China, Brazil, and India, could continue their financing programs.

Separately, the United States has engaged in efforts to negotiate export credit guidelines with China. During Chinese Vice President Xi Jinping's visit to the United States in February 2012, the United States and China announced that they would establish an International Working Group on Export Credits composed of export financing providers, with the goal of completing a new set of

---

[35] OECD, "New export credit rules will boost railway development and help countries achieve greener growth, OECD says," press release, September 1, 2014, http://www.oecd.org/trade/new-export-credit-rules-will-boost-railway-development-and-help-countries-achieve-greener-growth-oecd-says htm.

[36] AidData, Tracking Chinese Development Finance to Africa; Kevin P. Gallagher, Amos Irwin, and Katherine Koleski, *The New Banks in Town: Chinese Finance in Latin America*, Inter-American Dialogue, March 2012, http://www.thedialogue.org/PublicationFiles/TheNewBanksinTown-FullTextnewversion.pdf.

---

export credit guidelines by 2014.[37] Since November 2012, the International Working Group has met several times. Discussions have focused on negotiating new guidelines for the ships and medical equipment sectors that would form the basis for horizontal, broadly-applicable guidelines; information exchanges on working group members' export credit practices and policies; and discussion on members' negotiating positions.[38] Given the complexity of the issues at hand, there is speculation over whether the 2014 goal will be met.

Selected Issues for Congress

Status of Ex-Im Bank Authority

Over time, Congress has debated the acceptability of federal support for U.S. exports, with the debate growing more complex as the global marketplace has become more competitive. Members of Congress hold a range of views regarding how to address the status of Ex-Im Bank's authority, which is set to expire at the close of business on September 30, 2014, unless Congress takes action. Certain policy options are discussed below.

Renewal of Authority

Some Members of Congress have called for reauthorization of Ex-Im Bank in its current form— as an independent federal government agency that serves as the official ECA of the United States. Among those that favor a renewal of the Bank's charter, some may call for a "clean reauthorization," while others may support a reauthorization that includes certain reforms to the Bank, such as to its policies or risk management practices (see discussion below).[39]

Proponents of Ex-Im Bank reauthorization hold that the Bank is critical in supporting U.S. jobs and U.S. exports by addressing market failures (such as imperfect information and barriers to entry) and leveling the playing field by countering foreign government-backed export financing activity. They say that U.S. government backing of Ex-Im Bank activity can make certain transactions (e.g., for large, infrastructure projects or for small business exports) more commercially attractive by mitigating and diversifying risks, as well as provide the Bank leverage to guarantee repayment or recover assets in a way not available to the private sector. The Administration's legislative proposal submitted in April 2014 requests a five-year renewal of the Bank's current authority.

---

[37] Australia, Brazil, Canada, China, the European Union, India, Indonesia, Israel, Japan, New Zealand, Norway, South Africa, South Korea, Switzerland, Turkey, Russia, and the United States.

[38] *Treasury Report to the Committee on Banking, Housing, and Urban Affairs of the Senate and the Committee on Financial Services of the House of Representatives on Export Credit Negotiations*, December 2013.

[39] For example, H.R. 4950 (Heck), introduced in the 113th Congress, would renew Ex-Im Bank's authority for seven years and increase its exposure cap incrementally to $175 billion for FY2021. Also, in the 113th Congress, draft legislation introduced for the purposes of discussion (Campbell) in the House would renew Ex-Im Bank's authority for three years; reduce its exposure cap incrementally to $95 billion for FY2017; and institute a number of reforms to the Bank's structure, policies, and practices with the goal of reducing U.S. taxpayer exposure, improving risk management, and ensuring that the Bank remains a "lender of last resort." See http://campbell.house.gov/uploads/ CAMPBE_016_xml%20Second%20Draft.pdf.

Critics of Ex-Im Bank may concede that the Bank's programs can help individual firms, but hold that its programs shift production among sectors within the economy and do not add permanently to the overall level of U.S. exports.[40] They contend that the Bank competes with, or crowds out, private sector activity; the Bank picks "winners and losers" through its support and operates as a form of "corporate welfare;" poses a risk to taxpayers through its activities; and that the private sector is more efficient and better suited than the federal government to finance exports. Critics of the Bank also may call for intensified U.S. efforts through the OECD, as well as other venues, to eliminate all government-backed export credit activity internationally.

If Congress chooses to reauthorize Ex-Im Bank, a related issue is the length of time to extend the Bank's authority. A shorter renewal period, requiring reauthorizations more often, could provide more opportunity for more active congressional oversight of the Bank's activities (though Congress can weigh in on Ex-Im Bank anytime). In contrast, a longer renewal period or a permanent extension of authority could enhance the Bank's ability for long-term planning and provide more assurance to U.S. exporters, foreign buyers, and lenders of Ex-Im Bank's services. In the most recent reauthorization, passed in 2012 (P.L. 112-122), Congress extended the Bank's authority for about two years through FY2014. The length of recent longer-term reauthorizations was typically four or five years.[41]

Lapse in Authority

Some Members of Congress support allowing Ex-Im Bank's authority to expire. Some may favor a temporary expiration until consensus is reached on certain reforms that should be required of the Bank, while others may call for a permanent expiration. Congress could allow Ex-Im Bank's authority to expire by taking no action, or alternatively, by passing legislation that, for instance, sets specific parameters for a wind-down in its functions.[42] Uncertainty over whether Congress will renew Ex-Im Bank's authority reportedly has led, in some instances, to foreign buyers selecting other suppliers over U.S. suppliers for certain export contracts, out of concern about financing.[43]

Generally speaking, according to Ex-Im Bank, if its authority were to lapse, no new commitments (including new loan, guarantee, or insurance transactions) could be approved by its Board of Directors or under delegated authority, but prior obligations (including disbursements on already-approved final commitments) would continue. The Bank would continue to make expenditures in its operations (including salary, rent, etc.), while developing a plan for orderly liquidation.[44] It is unclear what form a liquidation plan would take. The primary statutory basis for Ex-Im Bank's activities under a lapse in authority is found in its charter in 12 U.S.C. §635f (see **text box**).

---

[40] Critics may point to a combination of domestic macroeconomic factors and global economic developments that influence a nation's export levels in the long-run, in other words, supply and demand, reflecting world economic forces.

[41] For example, the 2002 reauthorization act (P.L. 107-189) extended Ex-Im Bank's authority for four years through FY2006, and the 2006 reauthorization act (P.L. 109-438) renewed its authority for five years through FY2011.

[42] For example, H.R. 2263 (Amash) and S. 1102 (Lee), introduced in the 113th Congress, propose a termination of the Bank three years after the act's enactment.

[43] Lauren Airey, "Manufacturers Testify Before House Ex-Im Panel," National Association of Manufacturers (NAM), April 9, 2014, http://www.shopfloor.org/2014/04/manufacturers-testify-before-house-ex-im-panel/31055.

[44] CRS electronic communication with Ex-Im Bank, May 1, 2014.

---

12 U.S.C. §635f. Termination date of Bank's functions; exceptions; liquidation

Export-Import Bank of the United States shall continue to exercise its functions in connection with and in furtherance of its objects and purposes until the close of business on September 30, 2014, but the provisions of this section shall not be construed as preventing the bank from acquiring obligations prior to such date which mature subsequent to such date or from assuming prior to such date liability as guarantor, endorser, or acceptor of obligations which mature subsequent to such date or from issuing, either prior or subsequent to such date, for purchase by the Secretary of the Treasury or any other purchasers, its notes, debentures, bonds, or other obligations which mature subsequent to such date or from continuing as a corporate agency of the United States and exercising any of its functions subsequent to such date for purposes of orderly liquidation, including the administration of its assets and the collection of any obligations held by the bank.

Beyond the specific impact of a lapse on Ex-Im Bank's day-to-day functions, there is broader debate about its implications for the U.S. economy in the long-term, with stakeholders' positions based on their views of the validity of Ex-Im Bank's rationales, i.e., to fill in gaps in private sector financing and offset competition from foreign ECAs. From one perspective, the absence of Ex-Im Bank financing could adversely affect particular U.S. firms or their employees that use Ex-Im Bank support in cases where they face difficulty accessing financing from the private sector at competitive terms.[45] From another perspective, there are doubts over whether the absence of Ex-Im Bank support would affect the overall level of exports and employment in the United States.[46] Given the various factors that affect U.S. export and employment levels, it may be difficult to determine the precise impact of the presence or absence of Ex-Im Bank financing on the U.S. economy in the long-run.

In terms of competitiveness, supporters of the Bank argue that, without Ex-Im Bank financing, it may be difficult for certain U.S. companies to compete for export contracts on a "level playing field" with foreign competitors that receive support from their government-backed ECAs or may lead to U.S. sourcing in overseas markets. They argue that a lapse in Ex-Im Bank's authority would amount to "unilateral disarmament," given continued operations by other countries of their ECA programs—for many of whom exports constitute a larger part of the national economy and ECAs are a core part of their national export strategies.[47] Critics argue that allowing the Bank's authority to lapse would provide the United States with an opportunity to lead by example in efforts to eliminate government-backed ECA programs internationally, and enable the United States to focus on what they view as more effective ways to boost U.S. exports, such as through U.S. tax reform or the negotiation and enforcement of international trade agreements.[48]

---

[45] For example, see discussion in U.S. Congress, Senate Committee on Banking, Housing, and Urban Affairs, *Continuing Oversight of the Recent Activities of the Export-Import Bank and the Critical Need to Reauthorize the Bank's Charter*, 112th Cong., 2nd sess., April 17, 2012, S. Hrg. 112-585.

[46] For example, see Heritage Action for America publications, such as Zack Slingsby, *Export-Import Bank Authorization*, Heritage Action for America, April 10, 2014, http://heritageaction.com/2014/04/export-import-bank-reauthorization/.

[47] U.S. Chamber of Commerce, *The Export-Import Bank of the United States: Its Impact on U.S. Competitiveness, Exports, and Jobs*, October 2013, https://www.uschamber.com/file/8234/download.

[48] For instance, see Sallie James, *Ending the Export-Import Bank*, CATO Institute, October 2012, http://www.downsizinggovernment.org/export-import-bank.

Reorganization of Functions

Reorganization of Ex-Im Bank's functions may be considered as an alternative to reauthorization or a lapse in authority. Motivations could include an interest in increasing the effectiveness and efficiency of government export promotion services, reducing their costs, and eliminating duplicative activities.[49] Various reorganization proposals have been considered over time. These have included proposals to consolidate certain trade and export finance functions of various government agencies into a "Department of Trade." In recent years, the reorganization debate has been renewed with President Obama's proposal in 2012 to reorganize the business- and trade-related functions of Ex-Im Bank and certain other federal entities into one department, a proposal reiterated in the President's FY2015 budget request.[50]

Trade reorganization discussions have rekindled policy debates about whether reorganization would reduce costs and improve the effectiveness of trade policy programs, or undermine the effectiveness of federal agencies, given their differing missions, and result in the creation of larger, more costly bureaucracy. While some stakeholders argue that consolidation of trade functions would result in more streamlined federal export assistance, others contend that it may result in federal services that are not responsive to the specific needs of certain exporter groups. Reorganization discussions also have renewed debates about whether overlap in services provided by federal government agencies constitutes duplication or the use of the same or similar tools to meet different goals.

Exposure Limit

If Congress decides to reauthorize Ex-Im Bank, it may consider whether to revise the Bank's exposure cap. When Congress established the Bank as an independent agency in 1945, it authorized a limit on the Bank's outstanding aggregate credit and insurance authority that was no greater than three and one-half times the Bank's authorized stock of $1 billion.[51] Since then, Congress has periodically raised the Bank's exposure cap (see **Table 5**).

---

[49] For a general discussion of the issue, see CRS Report R42555, *Trade Reorganization: Overview and Issues for Congress*, by Shayerah Ilias Akhtar. For an example of possible duplication concerns with respect to Ex-Im Bank, see CRS Report R43155, *Small Business Administration Trade and Export Promotion Programs*, by Sean Lowry.

[50] The White House, "Government Reorganization Fact Sheet," press release, January 13, 2012, http://www.whitehouse.gov/the-press-office/2012/01/13/government-reorganization-fact-sheet; and Office of Management and Budget (OMB), *Budget of the United States Government, Fiscal Year 2015*, "Creating a 21st Century Government" section, p. 39, http://www.whitehouse.gov/omb/budget/Overview.

[51] Ex-Im Bank initially was capitalized with a stock of $1 billion in 1934.

Table 5. Legislative Changes to the Export-Import Bank's Limit on Outstanding Aggregate Credit and Insurance Authority

Year	Legislation	New Limit Resulting from Legislation
1945	P.L. 79-173	Three and one-half times the authorized stock of $1 billion
1951	P.L. 82-158	Four and one-half times the authorized stock of $1 billion
1954	P.L. 83-570	$5 billion
1958	P.L. 85-424	$7 billion
1963	P.L. 88-101	$9 billion
1968	P.L. 90-267	$13.5 billion
1971	P.L. 92-126	$20 billion
1975	P.L. 93-646	$25 billion
1978	P.L. 95-630	$40 billion
1992	P.L. 102-429	$75 billion
2002	P.L. 107-189	Incremental increases in limit to $100 billion[a]
2012	P.L. 112-122	Incremental increase in limit to $140 billion, contingent on certain requirements[b]

Source: U.S. Code notes; Lexis Nexis; and Jordan Jay Hillman, *The Export-Import Bank at Work* (Westport 1982).

a. The 2002 reauthorization (P.L. 107-189) increased the Bank's exposure cap to $80 billion in FY2002, $85 billion in FY2003, $90 billion in FY2004, $95 billion in FY2005, and $100 billion in FY2006.

b. The 2012 reauthorization act (P.L. 112-122) increased the Bank's exposure cap to $120 billion in FY2012, $130 billion in FY2013, and $140 billion in FY2014—with the increases for FY2013 and FY2014 contingent on the Bank maintaining a "default rate" of less than 2% and on submitting various reports.

The 2012 reauthorization act increased the Bank's exposure cap from the previous limitation of $100 billion incrementally to $140 billion in FY2014, with the increase in the exposure cap contingent on the Bank maintaining a default rate of less than 2% and on meeting various reporting requirements. The Administration's legislative proposal submitted in April 2014 to reauthorize the Bank requests an incremental increase of the Bank's exposure cap to $160 billion in FY2018. Some stakeholders favor increasing Ex-Im Bank's exposure cap, based on its role in supporting U.S. exports. Others favor maintaining or reducing the exposure cap, based on concerns over Ex-Im Bank's ability to prudentially manage its growing portfolio (see discussion below).

Ex-Im Bank Policies

Ex-Im Bank's policies could be part of the reauthorization debate. Congress could choose to pass a "clean reauthorization" that introduces no major changes to the Bank's policies. Proponents may argue that Congress has struck a fair balance among the various stakeholder interests—such as business and labor interests—in its present requirements of Ex-Im Bank and that adjustments to this balance are unwarranted. However, a number of long-standing debates concerning the Bank's policies remain. Should Congress consider revisions to Ex-Im Bank's policies, at issue is the extent to which potential changes would: (1) balance Ex-Im Bank's core mission to boost U.S. exports and jobs with supporting other policy interests; and (2) compare to the policies of foreign

ECAs, which may have different mandates and priorities, but nevertheless serve as competitors to Ex-Im Bank. Certain policies that may be debated are summarized below.

Domestic Content

The OECD Arrangement contains no specific guidelines regarding content requirements, which relate to the amount of domestic and foreign content (e.g., labor, materials, and overhead costs) associated with the production of an export. Each ECA generally establishes its own guidelines in this area.

Ex-Im Bank bases its content policy on its congressional mandate to support U.S. jobs and views content to be "a proxy to evidence support for U.S. jobs."[52] The policy is intended to encourage U.S. companies to maximize their sourcing of U.S. content. However, Ex-Im Bank recognizes that U.S. export contracts may contain goods and services that are foreign-originated, and it allows financing support for such contracts, subject to certain restrictions and limitations. Under its content policy, for all medium- and long-term transactions, Ex-Im Bank limits its support to the *lesser* of: (1) 85% of the value of all goods and services contained within a U.S. supply contract; or 100% of the U.S. content of an export contract. In effect, the Bank requires a minimum of 85% U.S. content and a maximum of 15% foreign content for an export contract to receive the fullest extent of financing available by the Bank. If the foreign content exceeds 15%, the Bank's support would be reduced proportionally.[53] For short-term export contracts, the minimum U.S. content requirement for full Ex-Im Bank financing is generally 50%.

In contrast to Ex-Im Bank, foreign ECAs generally have lower domestic content requirements and some even have no domestic content requirements. ECAs of other countries have revised their content policies to reflect the changing nature of manufacturing, including the rise of global supply chains and the sourcing of inputs from multiple countries (see **Table 6**).

In the 2012 reauthorization legislation, Congress required Ex-Im Bank to review its domestic content policy for medium- and long-term transactions to "examine and evaluate the effectiveness of the Bank's policy in maintaining and creating jobs in the [United States]; and in contributing to a stronger national economy through the export of goods and services" by taking into account various factors, including U.S. employment considerations and competitiveness to foreign ECAs. Following the review, Ex-Im Bank announced certain policy updates. For example, in an effort to increase U.S. services exporters' access to its financing, Ex-Im Bank provided clarification on how its content policy determines the eligibility of a U.S. services provider and a U.S. services contract, as well as how foreign-developed technology and the tools or equipment used to execute a services contract are treated on a content basis. According to Ex-Im Bank, it made no changes to its underlying content policy with these clarifications.

In the past, some stakeholders have argued that the Bank's definition of national content does not take into account "the high value U.S. jobs in R&D [research and development], supply chain management, software design engineering, business development, and marketing, IP [intellectual

---

[52] Ex-Im Bank, *2013 Competitiveness Report*, June 2014, p. 92.

[53] See Ex-Im Bank's content policies for more details: http://www.exim.gov/products/policies/foreign_medium-long.cfm.

property] support, branding, and profit,"[54] which have been considered as limitations to U.S. service providers' ability to use Ex-Im Bank financing.

Table 6. Foreign Content Requirements of Selected Country ECAs

Country	Maximum Allowable Foreign Content to Receive Full Medium- and Long-Term Financing
Australia	15%
Canada	Support will be given if the transaction benefits national interest
France	40%; however, may allow more foreign content in transactions that advance strategic/national interests
Germany	30% combined local and foreign (non-domestic) content; however may allow more non-domestic content in transactions that advance strategic/national interests
Italy	Support will be given if the transaction benefits national interest
Japan	70%; however, foreign content may be higher on a case-by-case basis
United States	15%
United Kingdom	80%; however, may allow more foreign content in transactions that advance strategic/national interests

Sources: Ex-Im Bank, *Report to the U.S. Congress on Export Credit Competition and the Export-Import Bank of the United States, For the Period January 1, 2013 through December 31, 2013,* June 2014; meeting with Ex-Im Bank officials, May 5, 2011; House Committee on Financial Services, Subcommittee on International Monetary Policy and Trade, *The Role of the Ex-Im Bank in U.S. Competitiveness and Job Creation,* opening statement by Chairman Gary Miller, 112th Cong., 1st sess., March 10, 2011; OECD, *Export Credit Financing Systems in OECD Member Countries and Non-Member Economies,* May 1, 2008; and Coalition for Exports through Employment document.

Notes: These data should not be considered definitive; rather, they are intended to give an idea of the range of ECA content requirements. ECAs may not apply their content requirements on an absolute basis, and may consider requests for export financing on a case-by-case basis or may apply flexibility to their content rules, for example, in terms of definition, percentage of foreign content, or interpretation of national benefit.

Given the proliferation of global supply chains and foreign ECA policies, many U.S. businesses continue to call for additional flexibility in Ex-Im Bank's content requirements. For example, industry proposals have included recommendations that Ex-Im Bank lower its domestic content requirement, such as to 50% (the policy for short-term financing); match the average among OECD countries; or adopt a policy similar to the European Union ECAs and "automatically cover non-U.S. content for U.S. FTA [free trade agreement] partners who offer reciprocity for U.S. content under their export credit agencies."[55] Other industry recommendations include Ex-Im Bank expanding the definition of domestic content to include, for instance, R&D or other elements that support high-value additions to the U.S. economy. However, labor groups tend to be concerned about the impact that lowering national content requirements may have on employment in the home country. From their point of view, reducing these requirements may result in an outsourcing of labor to other countries. Others counter that the current requirements

---

[54] U.S. Congress, House Committee on Financial Services, Subcommittee on International Monetary Policy and Trade, *Statement for the Record from the Coalition for Employment through Exports,* 112th Cong., 1st sess., March 10, 2011.

[55] U.S. Congress, House Committee on Financial Services, Subcommittee on International Monetary Policy and Trade, *Statement of Karan Bhatia, Vice President & Senior Counsel, International Law & Policy, General Electric,* 112th Cong., 1st sess., March 10, 2011. Also see Gary Clyde Hufbauer, Meera Fickling, and Woan Foong Wong, *Revitalizing the Export-Import Bank,* IIE, Number PB11-6, May 2011.

may induce firms to use other ECAs for alternative sources of financing, which may cause them to shift production overseas.

Economic Impact Analysis

Ex-Im Bank is required to have regulations and procedures to insure that full consideration is given to the extent that any loan or guarantee is likely to have an adverse effect on U.S. industries and U.S. employment.[56] These regulations and procedures are in support of the congressional policy that in authorizing any loan or guarantee the Board of Directors shall take into account any serious adverse effect of such loan or guarantee.[57] Furthermore, the Bank is prohibited from extending any loan or guarantee that would establish or expand the production of any commodity for export by any other country if the commodity is likely to be in surplus on world markets or the resulting production capacity will compete with U.S. production of a similar commodity and will cause "substantial injury" to U.S. producers of a similar commodity.[58] The Bank defines risk of substantial injury as the extension of a loan or guarantee that will enable a foreign buyer to establish or expand foreign production by an amount that is equal to or greater than 1% of U.S. production.[59] The same prohibition applies to loans or guarantees subject to U.S. trade measures, such as anti-dumping or countervailing duties.[60] However, these prohibitions shall not apply if the Board of Directors determines that the proposed transaction's short- and long-term benefits to U.S. industry and U.S. employment are likely to outweigh the injury to U.S. producers and U.S. employment of similar commodities.[61]

Like Ex-Im Bank, other G-7 ECAs have a broad mandate to support transactions that benefit their domestic economy, and base their decision to provide support on economic impact. However, in contrast to foreign ECAs, Ex-Im Bank is required by law to use an economic impact analysis to assess each transaction for potential adverse impact on U.S. industry, which can lead to a denial of financing.[62]

Among the key issues in the 2012 reauthorization debate was whether Ex-Im Bank's economic impact analysis sufficiently analyzes the potential impacts to U.S. industry of Ex-Im Bank transactions, including downstream effects (see **text box**). The 2012 reauthorization act required Ex-Im Bank to develop and make publicly available methodological guidelines to be used by the Bank in conducting economic impact analyses. In April 2013, Ex-Im Bank published revised economic impact analysis procedures and guidelines, including for aircraft exports.

Supporters of Ex-Im Bank maintain that the economic impact analysis requirements ensure that the Bank meets its congressional mandate. At the same time, some U.S. exporters are concerned that the economic impact policies may be overly burdensome, detract from its core mission to support U.S. exports and jobs, and not be competitive to the policies of other ECAs. Other critics

---

[56] 12 U.S.C. 635a-2.

[57] 12 U.S.C. 635(b)(1)(B).

[58] 12 U.S.C. 635(e)(1).

[59] See Ex-Im Bank, *Economic Impact Procedures and Methodological Guidelines*, April 2013, http://www.exim.gov/generalbankpolicies/economicimpact/.

[60] 12 U.S.C. 635(e)(2).

[61] 12 U.S.C. 635(e)(3).

[62] Ex-Im Bank, *2013 Competitiveness Report*, June 2014, p. 91.

continue to be concerned that the economic impact policy does not adequately take into account downstream effects of Ex-Im Bank support.

U.S. Airlines' Lawsuits Against the Ex-Im Bank

Debate about the economic impact of Ex-Im Bank activities has been driven in part by a charge by Delta Airlines, Hawaiian Airlines, and the Airline Pilots Association that Ex-Im Bank financing for Boeing aircraft exports to India and other countries has resulted in to an oversupply of airline seats that has had an adverse effect on their businesses. The group also has charged that Ex-Im Bank's economic impact analysis procedures are inconsistent with the Bank's charter. In 2011, operating through the Air Transport Association of America (ATAA), but with the express exclusion of most of the members of that association, Delta filed a legal challenge against Ex-Im Bank seeking an injunction on Ex-Im Bank loan guarantees to Air India. In July 2013, a federal appeals court rejected the airlines' request, but required Ex-Im Bank to explain how its approval of the transactions has complied with its statutory mandate.

According to Ex-Im Bank, its economic impact analysis adequately takes into account U.S. economic effects of transactions. From the Bank's perspective, a lack of Ex-Im Bank financing for an aircraft export contract may not deter a foreign airline carrier from buying aircraft; however, in the absence of Ex-Im Bank financing, a foreign aircraft manufacturer may win the deal over a U.S. aircraft manufacturer.

Delta, Hawaiian and APA filed three subsequent lawsuits against the Bank, all of which are currently pending. Initially, the plaintiffs claimed that Ex-Im Bank financing support for the purchase of U.S.-manufactured aircraft by foreign airlines provided more favorable financing terms than were available to U.S. airlines. The later lawsuits dropped this assertion and instead claimed that Ex-Im Bank financing provides more favorable financing terms than might otherwise be available to the foreign airlines, but not necessarily better than financing terms available to U.S. airlines.

U.S. companies may obtain financing from the ECAs of other countries. For example, Delta has used government-backed export financing for its purchases of airplanes, such as from Canada's Bombardier Inc. or Brazil's Embraer S.A.

Sources: "Airlines Press Ahead With Ex-Im Bank Lawsuit After Judge Denies Injunction," *Inside U.S. Trade's World Trade Online*, February 9, 2012; Josh Mitchell and Corey Boles, "Boeing, Delta Clash on Exports," *The Wall Street Journal*, March 16, 2012; Ted Reed, "Delta, Leader Of The U.S. Airline Industry, Challenges Boeing And Export-Import Bank," *Forbes*, April 13, 2014; and Ex-Im Bank.

Environmental Impact Analysis

Ex-Im Bank's charter authorizes the Bank to grant or withhold financing support after taking into account the potential beneficial and adverse environmental effects of goods and services for which Ex-Im Bank direct lending and guarantee support is requested. The Bank must conduct an environmental review of all transactions greater than $10 million. Recent developments in Ex-Im Bank's environmental policies related to high-carbon projects, including support for exports for coal-fired power plants, has been subject to congressional action (see **text box**). According to Ex-Im Bank, its Environmental and Social Due Diligence Procedures and Guidelines, Supplemental High Carbon Guidelines, and public disclosure requirements (e.g., tracking and publishing greenhouse gas emission data associated with projects) have expanded over time and remain more comprehensive than those of other OECD ECAs.[63] In addition, Ex-Im Bank faces competition from ECAs outside of the OECD, such as China, which tend to be less rigorous in their environmental requirements for financing than OECD countries.

Supporters of Ex-Im Bank's environmental policy argue that the Bank must balance U.S. exporting interests with environmental policy considerations, per its mandate. However, some

---

[63] Ex-Im Bank, *2012 Competitiveness Report*, June 2013, p. 75; and Ex-Im Bank, *2013 Competitiveness Report*, June 2014, p. 59.

U.S. exporters are concerned that Ex-Im Bank's environmental impact policies may be overly burdensome and detract from its core mission to support U.S. exports and jobs. From this standpoint, situations in which Ex-Im Bank denies financing for projects that do not meet environmental requirements are contrary to its mission because it may result in lost export and employment opportunities.

Recent Developments

Following the announcement of President Obama's Climate Action Plan, Ex-Im Bank's Board of Directors approved revisions to the Bank's Supplemental Guidelines for High-Carbon Projects In December 2013. As revised, the Supplemental Guidelines state that "the Bank will not provide support for exports of high carbon intensity plants, except for high carbon intensity plants that (a) are located in the world's poorest countries, utilize the most efficient coal technology available and where no other economically feasible alternative exists, or (b) deploy carbon capture and sequestration (CCS), in each case, in accordance with the requirements set forth in these Supplemental Guidelines." However, Section 7081(4)(C) of the FY2014 appropriations act (P.L. 113-76) prohibits the use of Ex-Im Bank funds, until September 30, 2014, and under certain conditions, for the enforcement of any rule, regulation, policy, or guideline implemented pursuant to the Supplemental Guidelines. While some stakeholders may be critical of the appropriations language from an environmental perspective, others may argue that it provides greater flexibility for Ex-Im Bank to more effectively meet its export and jobs mandate while also contributing to U.S. foreign policy goals with respect to development in the world's poorest countries.

Shipping

Ex-Im Bank's seaborne shipping policy is based on Public Resolution 17 (PR-17, approved March 26, 1934, by the 73rd Congress), whose purpose is to "support the U.S. strategic objective of maintaining a merchant marine sufficient to carry a substantial portion of its waterborne export and import foreign commerce."[64] Under the shipping policy, most products supported by the Ex-Im Bank must be transported exclusively on U.S. vessels (e.g., direct loans of any amount, guarantees above $20 million, and products with repayment periods of more than seven years). Under limited conditions, a waiver on this requirement may be granted on a case-by-case basis by the U.S. Maritime Administration (MARAD).

Supporters contend that maintaining U.S. flag vessels is "critical to U.S. national security" and "essential to maintaining a commercial U.S.-flag merchant marine."[65] They argue that, from a budgetary standpoint, cargo preference is a "highly cost efficient way" to support a privately-owned U.S.-flag commercial fleet. Because the goods will be shipped regardless of which ship carries them, and therefore the cost will be incurred regardless, "requiring that some of the cargoes be shipped on U.S.-flag vessels leverages that basic transportation expense to provide other benefits to the nation at a fraction of direct cost purchase." The concern under this view is that otherwise, the U.S. government would have to "duplicate sealift capacity at enormous expense with government-owned vessels."[66] These merchant U.S.-flag vessels are then available

---

[64] Ex-Im Bank, *Ex-Im Bank Policies: Shipping Requirements (MARAD)*, http://www.exim.gov/products/policies/shipping.cfm. Maritime Administration, *U.S.-Flag Waterborne Domestic Trade and Related Programs*, http://www.marad.dot.gov/ships_shipping_landing_page/domestic_shipping/Domestic_Shipping.htm. Codified as 46 U.S.C. 55304, by P.L. 109-304, October 6, 2006.

[65] U.S. Congress, House Committee on Financial Services, Subcommittee on International Monetary Policy and Trade, *Statement of USA Maritime*, Hearing on the Role of the Export-Import Bank in U.S. Competitiveness and Job Creation, 112th Cong., 1st sess., March 11, 2011.

[66] Ibid.

---

to transport U.S. troops and military equipment. Proponents also argue that the cargo preference requirements help to support the U.S. shipping industry and the employment of shipboard crew.

Critics of the shipping policy argue that "both U.S. strategic requirements and the global shipping market have changed dramatically."[67] U.S. business groups contend that the shipping requirements can make U.S. goods less competitive relative to foreign goods for a host of reasons. While one or more countries used to have similar shipping requirements in the past, the United States appears to be the only country that continues to impose such requirements.[68] There may also be capacity constraints because there are a limited number of U.S. bulk cargo carriers. According to lenders and exporters, the higher rates and the route scheduling challenges associated with shipping with U.S.-flagged vessels can make it difficult for them to use Ex-Im Bank support. For example, in one transaction with Ex-Im Bank, the cost of U.S. shipping reportedly was five times the cost of non-U.S. shipping,[69] raising competitiveness concerns. In addition, some businesses express concern about processing time and outcomes.[70]

Co-Financing

Ex-Im Bank introduced the co-financing program in 2001. Co-financing arrangements enable export credit financing from multiple ECAs. They allow goods and services from two or more countries to be marketed to a buyer under a single ECA financing package. According to U.S. exporters and lenders, co-financing arrangements allow Ex-Im Bank to participate with other ECAs on the non-U.S. content portion of an export contract. Otherwise, Ex-Im Bank would be limited to supporting the U.S. portion of the export contract and, from this view, the U.S. exporter may not win the sale because the ECA supported portion was insufficient or the terms and conditions were disadvantageous. In 2013, Ex-Im Bank conducted 51 co-financed transactions. According to the Bank, 99% of the volume, approximately $5 billion, involved some type of aircraft, with the exception of a medical equipment sale and a power transaction. The Bank states that, in most aircraft transactions, without co-financing, the exporter would not have been able to offer the maximum 85% support to its customers in one financing package.[71]

Following a review of its content policy, Ex-Im Bank announced changes to its co-financing arrangements. Under the revised co-financing policy, the Bank is willing to co-finance export contracts with a range of ECAs, if the proposed transaction complies with its statutory and policy requirements and benefits the U.S. economy. Some supporters call for more flexibilities in Ex-Im Bank's co-financing arrangements.

Tied Aid

Some U.S. exporters and lenders believe that Ex-Im Bank's tied aid policies may place them at a competitive disadvantage. U.S. exporters have expressed concern that increased tied aid activity by other countries, coupled with the more flexible tied aid rules of other ECAs, has threatened

---

[67] Coalition for Employment through Exports (CEE), *Ex-Im Bank 2011 Reauthorization: CEE Position Paper*.

[68] Ex-Im Bank, *2012 Competitiveness Report*, June 2013, p. 127.

[69] U.S. Congress, House Committee on Financial Services, Subcommittee on International Monetary Policy and Trade, *Statement for the Record from the Coalition for Employment through Exports*, 112th Cong., 1st sess., March 10, 2011.

[70] Ex-Im Bank, *2012 Competitiveness Report*, June 2013, p. 131.

[71] Ex-Im Bank, *2013 Competitiveness Report*, June 2014, p. 50.

certain U.S. exporter sales prospects. Some groups argue that the tied aid war chest funds should be increased and that the Bank should have more flexibility and authority in initiating tied aid to compete with foreign ECAs for export contracts, rather than limiting its use to a defensive tool. In some cases, it may be difficult for exporters and lenders to make a case for receiving matching support to counter foreign tied aid competition, because of challenges in "obtaining credible evidence of case-specific financing terms from non-OECD ECA competitors."[72]

Mandates Targeting Ex-Im Bank Activity to Specific Sectors

Congressional mandates that require the Bank to focus support on specific exports may raise a number of questions, including the following.

Should Congress mandate that Ex-Im Bank seek to finance specific types of exports? On one hand, congressional mandates may enable Ex-Im Bank to support strategic, high-growth U.S. economic sectors; U.S. exporters that may need the financing assistance the most (e.g., small businesses); and sectors where federal support can make the most difference (e.g., for renewable energy exports that rely on newer forms of technology and for which commercial banks may be unwilling to provide financing on their own because of actual or perceived risks). On the other hand, such targeted forms of export assistance may be viewed as a mechanism whereby the federal government determines "winners and losers" in the market, and, from this standpoint, may lead to economic distortions and harm other productive U.S. firms. Although such requirements give Congress a greater role in guiding Ex-Im Bank's activities, under this view, they may obscure the Bank's core mandate to support U.S. exports and employment.

To what extent has Ex-Im Bank been able to fulfill congressional mandates? On one hand, there is concern that the Bank has not been able to consistently meet its congressional mandates to support specific exports. Some critics express concern that Ex-Im Bank's prioritization of activities, allocation of resources to support policy goals, policies, and application process and approval system may limit its support for such policy goals. On the other hand, some stakeholders express concern that such mandates may not be feasible to achieve, based on market limitations, such as for renewable energy.[73] Given its demand-driven nature, Ex-Im Bank can make financing available for certain purposes, but its actual composition of financing portfolio depends on commercial interest and demand.

What is the appropriate measure of success? Debates over whether Ex-Im Bank is fulfilling its congressional mandates often has centered on small businesses. Some stakeholders may argue that the focus on the dollar value of Ex-Im Bank support to small businesses is misleading, because larger corporations naturally conduct business activity requiring greater amounts of support. In addition, the data may not reflect all of the small businesses who benefit from Ex-Im Bank services through their role in the supply chain, such as by supplying parts and services to larger companies that are the direct beneficiaries of Ex-Im Bank financing, or by operating at sub-levels of the supply chain and serving as "suppliers to the suppliers."[74] Others express concern

---

[72] Ex-Im Bank, *2012 Competitiveness Report*, June 2013, p. 105.

[73] For instance, see U.S. Congress, House Committee on Financial Services, *Ex-Im Bank Oversight: The Role of Trade Finance in Doubling Exports over Five Years*, Fred P. Hochberg, President and Chairman of the Export-Import Bank, 111th Cong., September 29, 2010.

[74] For example, see U.S. Chamber of Commerce Coalition Letter to Members of the United States Congress on Ex-Im Bank, February 13, 2012, https://www.uschamber.com/letter/coalition-letter. See also Coalition for Employment (continued...)

over the amount of Ex-Im Bank financing, by dollar value, that has been directed to large U.S. corporations that they believe are capable of shouldering the risks of exporting to developing countries.[75] For instance, some have criticized the fact that Boeing Corporation, a U.S. aerospace company, historically has been the single largest beneficiary of its support.[76] In addition, some critics do not make a distinction between large and small business support, remaining opposed to taxpayer funds being directed toward private benefits.

Risk Management and Financial Accounting

Congressional interest in Ex-Im Bank's financial soundness and risk management has been longstanding. It has been motivated, in part, by interest in the impact of Ex-Im Bank's activity on U.S. taxpayers, given that the Bank's activities are backed by the full faith and credit of the U.S. government. In recent years, Ex-Im Bank's growing exposure levels have heightened congressional scrutiny in its financial soundness and risk management practices.

The 2012 reauthorization act required Ex-Im Bank to monitor its default rate, report it on a quarterly basis to Congress, and to develop a plan to reduce the default rate if it exceeds 2% (sometimes called "the 2% rule"). The Bank's default rate as of March 31, 2014, was 0.211%.[77] Among other things, the 2012 act also required Ex-Im Bank to submit a written report to Congress and the Comptroller General containing: (1) a Business Plan estimating appropriate exposure limits for 2012, 2013, and 2014; and (2) an analysis of the potential for increased or decreased risk of loss to the Bank as a result of the estimated exposure limit.

Pursuant to the 2012 reauthorization act, the Government Accountability Office (GAO) published reports in March 2013 and May 2013 that reviewed Ex-Im Bank's risk management and reporting practices. The GAO found that Ex-Im Bank is moving toward a more comprehensive risk management framework and has made certain improvements over time, including enhancing credit loss modeling with qualitative factors. At the same time, the GAO also identified remaining weaknesses, considered further improvement to be needed based on the Bank's growing exposure level, and provided recommendations to Ex-Im Bank—all of which the Bank has reported accepting and working to implement (see **Table 7**). The Bank also notes other changes it has made in recent years, including appointing a Chief Risk Officer in 2013 to ensure prudential risk management, as well as establishing an Enterprise Risk Committee, modernizing its credit monitoring, creating a Special Assets unit to address emerging credit issues, expanding pro-active monitoring efforts, and improvement underwriting criteria.[78]

(...continued)

through Exports, *Supplier Study of 2011*, which analyzed the supply chains of five large companies (Bechtel, Boeing, Case New Holland, General Electric, and Siemens Power Corporation) that are the "exporters of record" for Ex-Im Bank, and identified more than 33,000 SMEs that supplied parts and services to these large companies for their exports.

[75] For example, see Sallie James, *Time to X Out the Ex-Im Bank*, CATO Institute, July 6, 2011, http://www.cato.org/publications/trade-policy-analysis/time-x-out-exim-bank.

[76] In FY2013, about 65% of Ex-Im Bank's authorizations of long-term guarantees, by dollar value, were for the sale of Boeing aircraft to foreign countries. CRS analysis of data in Ex-Im Bank annual reports.

[77] CRS electronic communication with Ex-Im Bank, May 30, 2014.

[78] U.S. Congress, Senate Committee on Banking, Housing, and Urban Affairs, *Oversight and Reauthorization of the Export-Import Bank of the United States*, Written Testimony of Fred P. Hochberg - President and Chairman of Ex-Im Bank, 113th Cong., 2nd sess., January 28, 2014.

Table 7. Risk Management: GAO Studies and Ex-Im Bank Action

Area	GAO Finding	GAO Recommendation	Ex-Im Bank Response
Exposure Forecasting	Ex-Im Bank's justification that the exposure limits it forecast in its 2012 Business Plan were appropriate has weaknesses, because the model is sensitive to key assumptions. Forecasting errors could have more significance since the Bank's exposure level is closer to its cap than historically, and could require, for example, the Bank to delay financing for projects, to avoid exceeding the limit.	The Bank should: (1) compare previous forecasts and key assumptions to actual results and adjust its forecast models to incorporate previous experiences; and (2) assess the sensitivity of the exposure forecast model to key assumptions and estimates and identify and report the range of forecasts based on its analysis.	The Bank agreed with the recommendation and stated it would incorporate these steps into preparation of updated and revised forecasts provided to Congress by September 30, 2013.
Stress Testing	The Bank has begun addressing the OIG's recommendations on portfolio stress testing, thresholds for portfolio concentrations, and risk management.	The Bank should report these findings to Congress.	The Bank agreed with the recommendation and intends to report stress test scenarios and results quarterly to Congress.
Risk Modeling	Improvements could be made in Ex-Im Bank's risk modeling, which uses historical data but may not use "best available data." The Bank's portfolio contains a large volume of recent transactions that have not reached their peak default periods.	Ex-Im Bank should assess whether it is using the "best available data" for adjusting loss estimates for longer-term transactions.	Ex-Im Bank agreed with the recommendation and said it would conduct an assessment as part of its 2013 reevaluation of its loss estimation model.
Financial Performance of Portfolio	Improvements could be made in the Bank's analysis of financial performance. For instance, the Bank does not have point-in-time performance data to compare performance of newer books of business with more seasoned books at comparable points in time.	Ex-Im Bank should retain point-in-time performance data to compare performance of newer and older business and enhance loss modeling.	Ex-Im Bank agreed to the recommendation and said it has begun retaining such data.
Sub-portfolio Reporting	Improvements could be made in the Bank's reporting of performance of sub-portfolios subject to congressional mandates (e.g., small business, renewable energy, and sub-Saharan Africa).	Ex-Im Bank should routinely report financial performance of subportfolios supporting congressional mandates.	Ex-Im Bank agreed with the recommendation and began reporting such information with its June 30, 2013, report to Congress.
Operational Risks	Ex-Im Bank faces potential operational risks because administrative budgets and staff levels have not kept pace with growth in portfolio.	The Bank should develop benchmarks to monitor and manage workload levels and provide Congress with additional information on resources associated with meeting mandated targets.	Ex-Im Bank concurred with both recommendations.

Source: CRS analysis of GAO, *Export-Import Bank: Recent Growth Underscores Need for Continued Improvements in Risk Management*, GAO-13-303, March 2013; and GAO, *Export-Import Bank: Additional Analysis and Information Could Better Inform Congress on Exposure, Risk, and Resources*, GAO-13-620, May 2013.

Notes: The findings and recommendations listed in this table are those of GAO. CRS does not take any position on these.

Nevertheless, debate continues over Ex-Im Bank's risk management and accounting practices, with key questions including the following.

Does Ex-Im Bank manage its risk adequately and balance it properly with other considerations? Supporters of Ex-Im Bank contend that the Bank has adequate systems and staffing in place to manage its risk and poses low risk to U.S. taxpayers. They argue that the Bank has a strong mandate to manage risk under its charter, which requires the Bank's transactions to have a "reasonable assurance of repayment" and for the Bank to have reasonable provisions for losses. They further note Ex-Im Bank's low default rate and high recovery rate.[79] Critics hold that there are weaknesses in the Bank's risk governance and question the methodology used to calculate Ex-Im Bank's expected losses and contributions to the Treasury. They express concern that the Bank's growing exposure and concentrations in that exposure, such as in aircraft, pose a risk to U.S. taxpayers and the federal budget, and point to certain findings in studies by the GAO and Ex-Im Bank's own Office of Inspector General (OIG) over time.[80]

Other stakeholders caution that the Bank may be becoming too risk-averse. Of particular interest has been heightened credit standards, including higher collateral requirements, introduced by Ex-Im Bank for its medium-term program, whose default rate is higher than that of Ex-Im Bank's overall portfolio.[81] These tighter standards have been associated with a decrease in Ex-Im Bank medium-term lending in recent years,[82] and have raised concerns about the appropriate balance in Ex-Im Bank's risk management with its overall mandate to support U.S. exports.

Does Ex-Im Bank have adequate human capital to prudentially manage its growing portfolio? Supporters contend that the Bank, with around 400 full-time equivalents in FY2013, is effective and efficient, and that in areas where weaknesses in risk management have been identified, the Bank is taking corrective measures, such as increasing resources devoted to due diligence and asset monitoring. Critics argue that the Bank does not have enough expertise devoted to underwriting and due diligence. They point to an assertion by Ex-Im Bank's OIG in 2012 that, "Ex-Im Bank's current risk management framework and governance structure are not commensurate with the size, scope, and strategic ambitions of the institution."[83]

Is the cost of federal credit by Ex-Im Bank appropriately priced? Some stakeholders argue that rules under the Federal Credit Reform Act (FCRA) may understate the cost of loan programs managed by federal credit agencies, and express interest in moving to a fair value system of accounting. As previously noted, under FCRA's rules, budget estimates are calculated by discounting them using the rates on U.S. Treasury securities with similar terms to maturity—which traditionally have been considered risk-free—and are below rates on commercial loans. In

---

[79] For example, see NAM, *Facts on the Export-Import (Ex-Im) Bank*, http://www.nam.org/~/media/ 5AF9A722407E46D6A1264820B2208860.ashx.

[80] For example, see Diane Katz, *U.S. Export-Import Bank: Corporate Welfare on the Backs of Taxpayers," The Heritage Foundation*, April 11, 2014, http://www.heritage.org/research/reports/2014/04/us-exportimport-bank-corporate-welfare-on-the-backs-of-taxpayers.

[81] GAO, *Export-Import Bank: Additional Analysis and Information Could Better Inform Congress on Exposure, Risk, and Resources*, GAO-13-620, May 2013, p. 22.

[82] Based on data from Ex-Im Bank annual reports.

[83] Ex-Im Bank, OIG, *Semiannual Report to Congress, April 1, 2013 to September 30, 2013*, p. 11, http://www.exim.gov/oig/upload/OIG_Report_FA13_508.pdf.; and Ex-Im Bank, OIG, *Report on Portfolio Risk and Loss Reserve Allocation Policies*, OIG-INS-12-02, September 28, 2012, http://www.exim.gov/oig/upload/Final-20Report-20Complete-20Portfolio-20Risk-20120928-1.pdf.

---

contrast, fair value accounting would factor in the market risk, which the non-partisan Congressional Budget Office (CBO) says "provides a more comprehensive measure of federal costs." On a fair value basis, Ex-Im Bank's programs may be less profitable than under FCRA rules. According to CBO's analysis, in FY2013, under FCRA, Ex-Im Bank generated a negative subsidy of $1 billion (i.e., "profit"). In contrast, under fair value, the negative subsidy is estimated to be much lower, at $0.1 billion.[84] In a separate study, CBO estimated that between FY2015-2024, Ex-Im Bank's activities would generate a negative subsidy of $14 billion under FCRA (i.e., budgetary savings), but would generate $2 billion in positive subsidy during this period on a fair value basis (i.e., budgetary costs).[85] However, some stakeholders question the assumptions used by CBO in its methodology, including for risk, and assert that CBO's assumptions overlook Ex-Im Bank's actual record, for example, in terms of its contributions to the U.S. Treasury and low default rate.[86]

Effectiveness of International Rules on Government-Backed Export Credit Activity

Stakeholders have debated whether the OECD Arrangement on Officially Supported Export Credits is effective in leveling the playing field for exporters in the current trading environment. By some estimates, the OECD Arrangement has saved U.S. taxpayers $800 million annually. According to the Office of the U.S. Trade Representative, the minimum interest rate rules set by the OECD Arrangement limit subsidized export financing and reduce competition based on below-cost interest rates and long repayment terms by ECAs, and the minimum exposure fees for country risks also reduce costs. The further leveling of the playing field created by the OECD tied aid disciplines is estimated by USTR to have boosted U.S. exports by $1 billion a year.[87]

At the same time, there are growing questions about the relevance of the OECD Arrangement and its effectiveness, particularly in light of the growing official export credit activity of non-OECD members such as China, Brazil, and India, who are not obligated to comply with the OECD limitations on the terms and conditions of export credit activity and may not be "playing by the rules."[88] To the extent that the ECAs of China and other non-OECD countries provide financing on terms that are more advantageous than those allowed within the OECD Arrangement, Ex-Im Bank and other OECD export credit agencies may find it difficult to compete with such export credit programs. Concerns about the effectiveness of the OECD Arrangement are further heightened due to unregulated financing being conducted by OECD member countries, such as through market windows, which are not subject to the Arrangement.

---

[84] Congressional Budget Office (CBO), *Fair-Value Estimates of the Cost of Federal Credit Programs in 2013*, June 2012, http://www.cbo.gov/sites/default/files/cbofiles/attachments/06-28-FairValue.pdf.

[85] CBO, *Fair-Value Estimates of the Costs of Selected Federal Credit Programs for 2015 to 2024*, May 2014, http://www.cbo.gov/sites/default/files/cbofiles/attachments/45383-FairValue.pdf.

[86] For example, see Gary Clyde Hufbauer, *"The [Export-Import] Bank Loses Almost $200 Million a Year." Really?*, IIE, RealTime Economic Issues Watch, May 13, 2014, http://blogs.piie.com/realtime/?p=4311; and Christopher Wenk, *A Fair Accounting of the Ex-Im Bank's Benefits and Costs*, U.S. Chamber of Commerce, May 29, 2014, https://www.uschamber.com/blog/fair-accounting-ex-im-bank-s-benefits-and-costs.

[87] Office of the U.S. Trade Representative, *The Organization for Economic Cooperation and Development (OECD)*, http://www.ustr.gov/trade-agreements/wto-multilateral-affairs/oecd.

[88] Thought not a member of the OECD, Brazil is a participant of the OECD Aircraft Sector Understanding.

Congress could examine and seek to strengthen the international disciplines guiding ECA activity, to reflect current trends in ECA activity by both developed and developing countries. For example, Congress could direct the United States to encourage greater engagement by the OECD with non-OECD emerging market economies on official export credit activity; negotiate rules in the OECD that limit government-backed export credit financing in other developed countries; or pursue a greater role for the WTO in disciplining international ECA activity. On one hand, such efforts may help to level the playing field for U.S. exporters by reducing trade-distorting export credit competition and associated economic losses. On the other hand, changes to the international export credit rules, if achieved, may be slow to materialize, given the complex nature of multilateral and plurilateral negotiations. In addition, developing high-standard, comprehensive rules that cover both developed and developing countries may be a challenge.

Rather than strengthening international rules, others have called for renewed efforts by the U.S. Treasury to negotiate to eliminate all government-backed export financing internationally.[89] This perspective often is found with critics of Ex-Im Bank, while supporters of the Bank contend that even if all countries agree to eliminate government-backed export credit activity, there would still be a need for Ex-Im Bank to fill in gaps in private sector financing due to market failures.

Congressional Outlook

While congressional views on Ex-Im Bank differ, historically, Congress has reauthorized Ex-Im Bank on a bipartisan basis, including by voice vote in the House and unanimous consent in the Senate and with support from both Republican and Democrat Administrations. In the 112th Congress, discussion of whether to reauthorize Ex-Im Bank and raise its exposure cap, among other issues, dovetailed with debates about the agency's role in supporting U.S. exports and the appropriate size and scope of the U.S. government. The changing export finance landscape, including the international financial crisis and the growth of government-backed export financing being conducted by emerging markets, as well as increased questions about Ex-Im Bank's financial soundness and risk management, have intensified congressional interest in Ex-Im Bank. Many of these issues continue to be focal points in the Ex-Im Bank reauthorization debate in the 113th Congress.

---

[89] Recent developments in U.S. Treasury export credit negotiations are detailed in *Treasury Report to the Committee on Banking, Housing, and Urban Affairs of the Senate and the Committee on Financial Services of the House of Representatives on Export Credit Negotiations*, December 2013.

Appendix. International Government-Backed Export Credit Activity

Table A-1. New Medium- and Long-Term Official Export Financing Volumes for Selected ECAs,
2007-2013

Billions of U.S. Dollars

Country	2007	2008	2009	2010	2011	2012	2013
OECD ECAs					110.7	126.0	97.9
G-7 Countries	34.6	43.7	64.0	70.2	74.0	80.2	60.0
Canada	0.5	1.5	2.0	2.6	1.9	1.9	1.9
France	10.1	8.6	17.8	17.4	15.9	13.0	9.5
Germany	8.9	10.8	12.9	22.5	16.7	21.6	22.6
Italy	3.5	7.6	8.2	5.8	8.0	5.4	5.4
Japan	1.8	1.5	2.7	4.9	5.9	3.9	2.1
United Kingdom	1.6	2.7	3.4	4.1	4.2	2.9	3.9
United States	8.2	11.0	17.0	13.0	21.4	31.3	14.5
Selected Other OECD ECAs					32.5	41.1	33.4
Austria					0.7	1.4	1.1
Denmark					2.2	3.9	3.8
Finland					3.1	1.8	2.3
Netherlands					2.9	2.2	3.2
Norway					3.0	2.2	2.8
South Korea					9.8	22.6	14.8
Spain					4.4	2.0	1.2
Sweden					6.3	5.1	4.2
Other OECD ECAs (Estimated)					4.2	4.7	4.5
Emerging Economies (non-OECD) ECAs	n/a	33.0	51.0	40.0	47.0	50.1	55.4
Brazil	0.6	0.2	6.1	3.5	4.8	2.7	4.1
China	n/a	24.0	40.4	31.3	36.0	42.2	45.5
India	8.4	8.8	4.5	5.4	6.2	5.3	5.1
Russia	n/a	n/a	n/a	n/a	0.0	0.0	0.7

Source: Data on export credit volumes from Ex-Im Bank, *Report to the U.S. Congress on Export Credit Competition and the Export-Import Bank of the United States, For the Period January 1, 2013 through December 31, 2013,* June 2014.

Notes: Data subject to analytic assumptions and limited by availability of information. Unregulated financing conducted by OECD ECAs may be omitted. Ex-Im Bank Competitiveness Reports have included data for G-7 ECAs for many years, and in 2012, expanded the scope of OECD ECAs assessed beyond the G-7 ECAs. Further refinements could occur.

Author Contact Information

Shayerah Ilias Akhtar
Specialist in International Trade and Finance
siliasakhtar@crs.loc.gov, 7-9253

Acknowledgments

The author would like to acknowledge Jamie Hutchinson's assistance with several of the graphics in this report.